SELECTED POEMS
OF JAMES MCGRATH

Also by James McGrath from Sunstone Press:

At the Edgelessness of Light, 2005
Speaking With Magpies, 2007
Dreaming Invisible Voices, 2009
Valentines and Forgeries, Mirrors and Dragons, 2011
The Sun is a Wandering Hunter, 2015
A Festival of Birds, 2017
Mixed Greens, 2019
A Temporary Silence, 2021

SELECTED POEMS OF JAMES MCGRATH

Selecting Poems Is Selecting Wild Flowers Is Selecting Poems

Selected by:

David Cloutier
Morgan Farley
Catherine Ferguson
Paulette Frankl
Dale Harris
James McGrath
Verma Nequatewa and Robert Rhodes
Cynthia West

Cover photograph: James McGrath in the wild flower fields of Silver City, New Mexico, Daniel Forest, Santa Fe, New Mexico, photographer. Back cover photograph: Ted Katz, Durham, Oregon.

Sunstone books may be purchased for educational, business, or sales promotional use. For information please write: Special Markets Department, Sunstone Press, P.O. Box 2321, Santa Fe, New Mexico 87504-2321.
Printed on acid-free paper
∞

Library of Congress Cataloging-in-Publication Data

Names: McGrath, James, 1928- author.
Title: Selected poems of James McGrath / selecting poems is selecting wild flowers is selecting poems.
Description: Santa Fe : Sunstone Press, [2022] | Summary: "Poems by a well-known Southwestern US writer and teacher"-- Provided by publisher.
Identifiers: LCCN 2022041149 | ISBN 9781632934581 (paperback)
Subjects: LCGFT: Poetry.
Classification: LCC PS3613.C497 S45 2022 | DDC 811/.6--dc23/eng/20220916
LC record available at https://lccn.loc.gov/2022041149

WWW.SUNSTONEPRESS.COM
SUNSTONE PRESS / POST OFFICE BOX 2321 / SANTA FE, NM 87504-2321 /USA
(505) 988-4418

James McGrath, drawing by Catherine Ferguson,
Galisteo, New Mexico, 2022.

DEDICATION

To the congenial, supportive members of Sunstone Press of Santa Fe, New Mexico, Jim Smith, Carl Condit, Lindsay Ahl, designer, and Vicki Ahl, former designer, who have graciously travelled with me on the nourishing, mysterious road of words, the road of publishing my poetry since 2005.

Thank you.
James McGrath

Poem For The Year of The Tiger: 2022

"Tiger, tiger,
  what are you hunting in your poems for 2022?"

"I am hunting for the metaphors for my verb, *peace*."

"Tiger, tiger,
  where in the jungle will you find such metaphors?"

"They may be hidden in the tree of life."

"Tiger, tiger,
  what are you hunting in your poems of peace?"

"I am hunting for the metaphors of my verb, *love*."

"Tiger, tiger,
  where in the veld will you find such metaphors?"

"They may be hiding at the edge of the greening grass."

"This is where you sharpen your claws, poet."

—James McGrath

CONTENTS

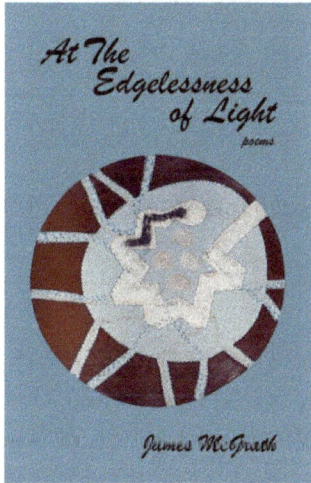

At The Edgelessness of Light, 2005

Selections by Morgan Farley:

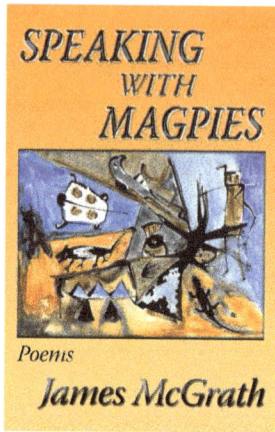

Speaking With Magpies, 2007

Selections by Cynthia West:

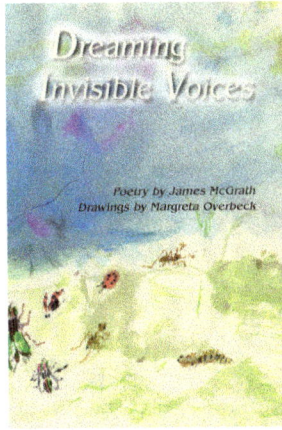

Dreaming Invisible Voices, 2009

Selections by David Cloutier:

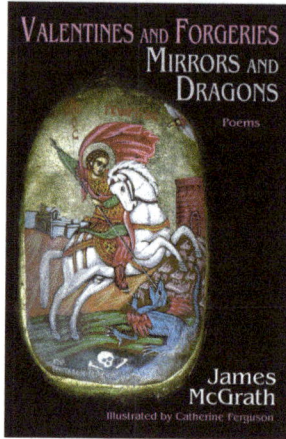

Valentines and Forgeries, Mirrors and Dragons, 2011

Selections by Ann Yeomans:

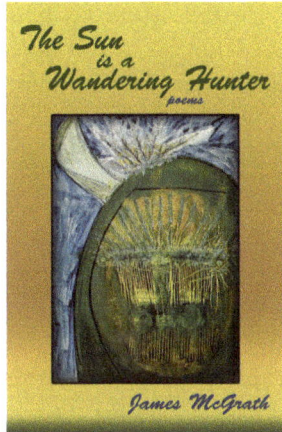

The Sun Is A Wandering Hunter, 2015

Selections by Verma Nequatewa and Robert Rhodes:

From *The Sun Is A Wandering Hunter*

From *Visions of Sonwai*

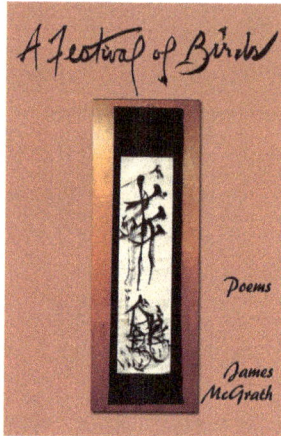

A Festival of Birds, 2017

Selections by Dale Harris:

(First Lines)

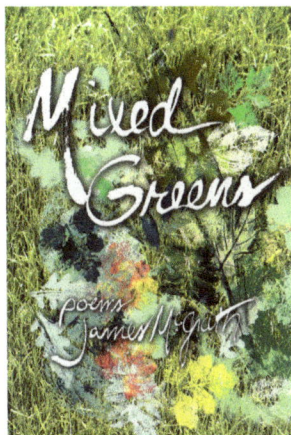

Mixed Greens, 2019

Selections by Catherine Ferguson:

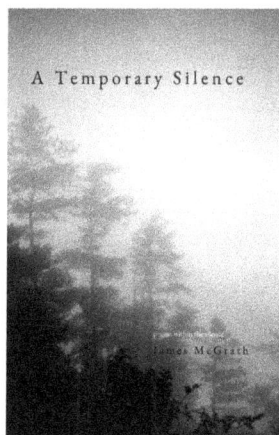

A Temporary Silence, 2021

Selections by Paulette Frankl:

Selections by the poet James McGrath:

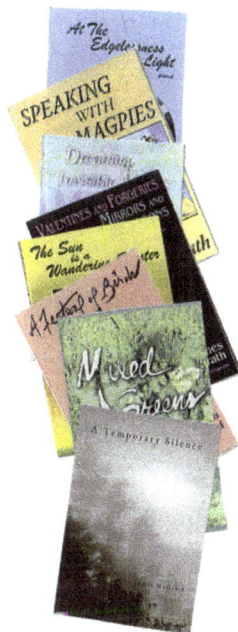

December 16, 1945

This is when it started: in Miss Cunningham's Literature 3 Class:
Lincoln High School, Tacoma, Washington, 1945.

We had been studying the dreamlike ballad, *The Rime of the Ancient
Mariner* by Samuel Taylor Coleridge. Our assignment was to write a poem
from a recent experience using a similar rhythm.

Jim McGrath
Literature 3 Per 4
December 16, 1945

After singing for five hours with the a capella choir at Fort Lewis, we finally came home and thence to bed. However dark it was, notes, chords, and even songs rang through our ears. We may hear a familiar note but when we hum it, always there was a discord.

These lines came to me as I was trying my best to sleep after this tiring day.

The room was dark,
And all about
There was an atmosphere
Of doubt.

I heard a note, 'twas a star
So clear, so bright — yet familiar
It rang and then departed.

2.

Jim Mc Grath
Literature 2 Per¹
December 16, 1945

I heard a note; it was as if a jewel.
So clear, so bright — yet familiar
I hummed — the spell was broken.

I heard a chord, 'twas as if a constellation
So familiar, so blended — yet unknown.
It rang and then departed.
I heard a chord, 'twas as if an organ.
So familiar, so blended — yet unknown
I hummed — the spell was broken.

I heard a song — a chord — a note
combined.
I knew it then! It was the world
Of which a part is mine.

The room was dark,
And all about
There was an atmosphere
Of doubt.

Original manuscript in James McGrath archives, in Special Collections;
University Libraries; University of Washington; Seattle, Washington
98195-2900.

After singing for five hours with the a cappella choir at Fort Lewis, we finally came home and thence to bed: However dark it was, notes danced before my eyes, chords, and even songs rang through my ears. Hearing a familiar note I would hum it, but always there was a discord.

These lines came to me as I was trying my best to sleep after this tiring day.

> The room was dark,
> And all about
> There was an atmosphere
> Of doubt.

I heard a note; it was a star
So clear, so bright—yet familiar
It rang and then departed.

I heard a note; it was a jewel
So clear, so bright—yet familiar
I hummed—the spell was broken.

I heard a chord, 'twas like as if a constellation
So familiar, so blended—yet unknown
It rang and then departed.
I heard a chord, 'twas like an organ
So familiar, so blended—yet unknown
I hummed—the spell was broken.

I heard a song—a chord—a note combined.

I knew it then! It was the world
Of which a part is mine.

> The room was dark,
> And all about
> There was an atmosphere
> Of doubt.

PREFACE

This writing a poem may have started with notes to Louise or Patty in Gray Junior High School and acknowledged in Miss Cunningham's Literature 3 class at Lincoln High School in 1945, when I was 17. Writing a poem has rarely stopped being the energy in the expression of my creative life.

Creating *Selected Poems of James McGrath* is an intimate community celebration. This to say, indispensable, caring members of the family of writers, poets, educators and artists I am on the journey with, have selected poetry from my eight books of poetry published by Sunstone Press of Santa Fe, New Mexico since 2005:

Morgan Farley
Cynthia West
David Cloutier
Ann Yeomans
Verma Nequatewa and Robert Rhodes
Dale Harris
Catherine Ferguson
Paulette Frankl

Because poems are interpreted differently by each person, poems are offered here as unique gifts, as essential heartbeats in my poet life of ninety-four years.

This offering of poems in the digital-virus-electronic life of the early 2020s is sharing unrehearsed views and voices, filtering light and darkness that declares memory with imagination and observation of the open spaces and closets to be essential for my survival and healing in the lull and turmoil.

Here are poems to take the mask away.

James McGrath

INTRODUCTION
by Joan Logghe

"Birds sing one song
Please remember me"

M ost selected poems have the poet choose from their own body of work. The refreshing decision to have nine poet friends each select ten of James McGrath's poems from each of eight books, gives a deeper experience and entry into the world he loves. It is the world that hears what the animals are saying, travels the beloved earth, and puts down roots along with the apple trees of his home in La Cieneguilla.

I met James years ago in my poetry class in the basement of Mothering Magazine where I was the poetry editor. I found him an engaging student—a hint of Gary Snyder, a bit of William Stafford, all three with Northwest vibes and sensibilities. Little did I know what a gentle force he already was and how strong he would become in his commitment to poetry.

Recently, after I met James to talk about this book, he stood on the curb waving me goodbye until I drove off, maybe a farewell tradition in a country where James had traveled. He's been to Ireland and Yemen, Japan and Korea, Saudi Arabia, and a year at Hopi. He has taught poetry and art internationally and delighted me with his ease and excellence. Delight may be the operative word in this collection.

James' relation to art has the quality of loving the creative more than ambition or ego. In his lifelong commitment to art he taught at the inception of IAIA, the Institute of American Indian Art, when Joy Harjo was a student, and now she's the Poet Laureate of the United States. James not only won the Living Treasures of Santa Fe designation, 2015 Passager Magazine Award, and the Poetry Gratitude Award from New Mexico Literary Arts, but embodies a true artist, living in La Cieneguilla where he famously hosted poetry readings in his orchard for a variety of poets.

James inhabits his body like a teenager, agile and younger than his 94 calendar years. Maybe it is because he spends time with the birds and the juicy pears. Or maybe he stays alive in his art because for years he has met four days a week to write with fellow poets by telephone long before remote was a thing.

I taught from James' poems to hundreds of school children who responded with enthusiasm, maybe because they heard the animals, spiders, and the wind speak too.

Rereading these poems, I have a renewed appreciation for their rich simplicity. James lets us into a life well lived. Through his work he shares his endless energy. I've met plenty of poets, but none with the sweet talent for living in the gift and sharing bees and frogs, flies and magpies, from the well of generosity that lives inside our Living Treasure, James McGrath.

"I think it's okay.
It's okay to say goodbye
as long as it's in a different language."—James McGrath

Joan Logghe served as Santa Fe Poet Laureate from 2010 to 2012. Her most recent books are *The Singing Bowl* (University of New Mexico Press), *Unpunctuated Awe* (Tres Chicas Books), and *Odes & Offerings: A Collaborative Exhibit of Poetry and the Visual Arts* (Sunstone Press).

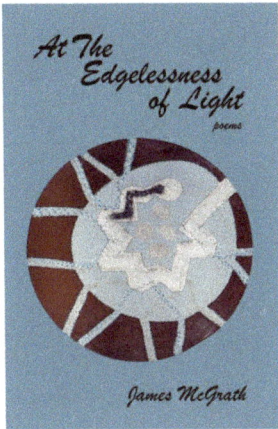

James McGrath

At the Edgelessness of Light, 2005
Selections by Morgan Farley

I had the great good fortune of hearing these early poems pour out of James in many places, from a writing circle in my living room to the Greek island of Leros to the flat roof of Yeats's stone tower. They felt ancient as Homer and fresh as the Irish dew. We were writing on the shores of Lily Lake when I asked him where his poems came from. He gazed up at the blue Colorado sky, murmured "from the edgelessness of light," and his first collection was born.

James is poet as magician, as shaman, so porous to the world he can shape shift into a magpie, a shadow, a stone. He ventures beyond metaphor into metamorphosis, becoming the things he loves. When we write together I feel him welcoming whatever wants to speak—dust or star, dream or memory, bearable or unbearable—with a love that makes me glad to be alive. It takes high courage to make a home for shadows and lightning in your own flesh. In his vibrant life and in these dazzling delicate poems James shows us how to weave the terrible with the tender until there are no edges to the light.

M organ Farley is an award-winning writer, psychotherapist, developmental editor and writing coach. She has been on a writing odyssey with James since 1994, when he sent her broadsides of his poems

after hearing her read. That happy impulse led to twenty-seven years of writing adventures at home and abroad, annual readings in the orchard, dream groups and writing groups and high teas for two. She gives thanks for the unfailing inspiration and support of a constant friend of the work and a true soul friend.

Morgan Farley with
James McGrath, 2002

In the Edgelessness of Light

Here in the brilliance of this place,
    where light flits from leaf to leaf,
    where light lies resting,
    vibrating on stilts of grass,
    its radiance pulling the shine
    from embarrassed stars,

here where light folds into fading petals
    of wild roses,
    where the feathered light
    of lost geese hovers in cottonwoods,
    its brightness polished by pollen and honey,

here is where I become a shadow in safety,
    retreating,
    leaving shields and spears behind,
    back to the beginning
    where the edgelessness of light
    flares across your face
    and I see you for the first time.

                17 July 2003
                Santa Fe, New Mexico

at the
edgelessness
of light

He was a Man Who Loved Oranges

He sat alone
    in a bed of ivy
    peeling oranges,
    his feet hidden
    in the shadows of flying blue jays.

I watched him tear open the film
    of orange skins
    with the sharpness of his eyes.
    Then piece by piece
    he made a mosaic,
    lining his silhouette
    with broken fruit.

He was a man who loved oranges.
The sweet juice ran in his memory.

His eyes were swollen
    with sprouting seeds.

His hands were stained
    and lined with pollen
    that left traces of butterflies
    in his passport.

There were traces of Neroli oil
    behind his ears
    from childhood,
    and when the moon
    went behind clouds
    on lonely nights
    auras of lightning bugs

circled his head
and sang songs
that made oranges blush.

I saw him take another orange,
press it to his ear,
listening.

His face showed pain
as if he heard
his father calling him.

He tossed the orange
into the air.
It floated,
glistening as the sun
glistens in fog.

From a pine tree
a blue jay called,
swooped,
speared the orange,
flew away,
carrying that orange man's father
down the cliff-side
to where sea stones
were waiting for storms.

That orange man
jumped from his bed of ivy,
flew after the jay
down the cliff-side.

The last I saw of him
he was breaking open
the skulls of sea kelp,
searching
for his lost orange.

He wanted to have a last word
    with his father
    so he could finish his poem.

        19 April 1999
        Esalen, Big Sur, California

Songs of My Uncle's Horse
—*for Martha Yates, my traveling friend*

He said,

> a horse is a horse
> only when it is touched.

He said,

> I see the shape of the wind
> when I see my horse run.

He said,

> when my horse is alone
> I see his loneliness go in search of itself.

He said,

> I see the gold in my horse's eyes.
> It is the same gold that lies
> at the tips of water in sunlight.

He said,

> my horse's mane
> is the winter grass blowing.

He said,

> my horse is the dance of time
> when he comes to me.

He said,

    the salty sweat of my horse
    is not bitter;
    it is sweet like the flight of bees.

He said,

    when I ride my horse
    it is without a saddle,
    it is without spurs;
    it is best without clothing of any kind
    so my horse and I
    become the arrow and the bow.

June 1998
Santa Fe, New Mexico
Published 2000: *Animals in Poetry*,
Soulspeak, Sarasota Theatre Press

Nasturtiums and Glue

When I walked into her room
        she was curled into a white ball.

Her gown white.
Her hair white.
Her skin pink, faded nasturtiums.

I whispered, "Mother, are you awake?
        Are you awake?"

She snapped open her pea-pod
        blue eyes. Smiled.

Did she know me?

We went down the hall to the lunchroom.

It smelled stale, like wet crackers.

We sat at a table in the company
        of two other ladies,
        white with nasturtium skin.

The mushroom soup was barely warm.

It tasted like the Lepage's glue
        from Fourth Grade.

                    February 2002
                    Santa Fe, New Mexico

At Coole Lake
     —*for Morgan Farley, my poet friend*

This stone I lean against is my father's back.

He sits aft in the boat,
          the oars beside us.

The tongue of the lake
          laps against our silence.

Birds at the edge of reeds and hemlocks
          forget we are there.
          They fly across our heads.

We bow and bend.

There are rainbow trout here
          and multicolored feelings
          between my father and me.

I feel them in the quietness
          of this place
          when our backs are one against the other,
          our silence lapping the bottoms of clouds,
          sinking under the waters of this lake.

The poles we hold in our hands,
          his points West,
          mine points East,
          their threaded lines lost
          beneath the surface of all things
          like the lines of our words.

This stone I lean against is impenetrable

as the days between my father and me:
dark, hard days.

The surface of this lake,
    like the surface of those days,
    is pitted with an indecipherable language
    that only a son
    may hear from his father,
    indecipherable because there were so few words.

Like the stone that I lean against here,
    there is no pattern.
    There is no edge to this stone
    that may fit it into the shape
    and shadow of the stone
    that sits next to it.

I would like to bring this stone for leaning
    to my home.

It is strong and rough.

The angle of it is comforting.

I can lean back, son-like,
    to hear clouds and time
    flowing from East to West
    like the silence between fishing poles.

This is my silence now.

I am the bait at the end of the fishing-line.

What I catch, I can put back into the waters
    or breathe into a pair of swans.

            11 June 2001
            Coole Lake, County Galway, Ireland

Son of the Hunter
in memory of Francis Anthony McGrath, my father

The deer hung his bronze head.
Dad stood me beside his bronzeness
    like a member of the family.

I let my picture be taken,
    my eyes wandering down his stretched
    hind legs tied with wire to the rafters,

my eyes wandering into the red opening
    that was once a hot stomach,

my eyes meeting the frosted stare
    of deer-eyes browned over
    with the last vision of pine-forest
    and rock-falls.

Even after the camera was put away
    and the hunters left the barn,
    my eyes continued to wander,
    to stop and stare
    at the great silence of coarse fur,
    the wide arching horns.

I wanted to crawl outside my eyes
    to curl up in the open circle
    of those wide horns,
    to be pierced as the deer had been pierced.

I wanted to feel the pain
    of that golden deer.

I wanted to run my teeth against
  the roughness of the horns
  as they entered his head,
  knobby and touched with his blood.

I wanted to be embroidered with his fur
  so I would never be cold again.

I wanted to animal,
  and I wondered how he cried
  when he fell off his mountain,
  and if I put my finger in the bullet-hole
  would he breathe again.

November 1992
Santa Fe, New Mexico
Broadside self-published Fall 1995
Published 2003: *Passager, A Journal
of Remembrance and Discovery*,
MaryAzrael and Kendra Kopelke, editors.

When No One Was Listening

All through my school years I stuttered;
     from kindergarten through college
     I stuttered.

He told me never to tell anyone
     what he did to me.
He told me never to say anything

So I hid in silence.
     In school I would whisper.
     Somehow, I could whisper.

I often got caught
     and spent many days in the cloakroom,
     that awful creosote-smelling cloakroom
     with galoshes and lunch sacks
     and damp woolen scarves.

I wrote a lot of notes to Jackie and Coral and Dick.
They were intercepted by those teachers
     in tight-fitting jersey dresses
     who sent messages home to say
     Jimmy must pay more attention in class.

Once in high school I wrote a poem that
     Miss Cunningham asked me, out loud,
     if she could read to the class.
I nodded, yes.
She must have decided that I couldn't
     read my own poem.
That poem was in Grade Eleven.

She never knew I had boxes of my voice
     from Grade One, Grade Two, Three,
     Four, Five, Six, Seven, 8, 9, and 10.
Even when Uncle Fred died,
     I still stuttered and kept silent
     and wrote poems.

I stopped stuttering that day
when my poem greeted me and said,
"I love you,"
     and no one was listening.

        February 1999
        Santa Fe, New Mexico
        Published 2000: *In Cabin Six, An Anthology*
        of Poetry by Male Survivors of Sexual Abuse,
        Jill Kuhn, editor, Impact Publishing

There is a River Running in the Blood of Him

There is a river running in the blood of him
    as he tumbles down the mountainside,
    rolling the stones aside,
    scattering birds.

A river running in the blood of him
    tosses his arms with the reeds and rushes
    in the greenest of thunders
    and the gold dust of rain.

A river running in the blood of him
    murmurs and purrs
    when he sleeps
    where he sleeps
    in the distant places without names.

Oh, the sound.
Oh, the whimper of a river running in the blood of him,
    frog voices dark,
    escaping as the moon rises
    on a coyote's wail.

Oh, the fury.
The river running in the blood of him
    calling for a response
    from the sun setting
    too early in his daylight.

Only the newest of moons can cup
    and hold the tears
    running in the blood of him.

September 2000
Santa Fe, New Mexico
Published 2001: *The Cancer Poetry Project,
Poems by Cancer Patients and Those Who Love Them,*
edited by Karin B. Miller, Fairview Press

Self-portrait
   —for Jain Kelain Middaugh, my daughter

In a college painting class
      I used palette knife and hot orange
      and blue oils on burlap.
      Then I was rougher, bolder,
      and more open,
      woven like burlap.

Now I am more grey and fading sunset darker.

During my fifteen years with the Indians
      I painted my portrait
      on a round canvas shield.
      It was full of feathers and bird tracks,
      and the back of the shield
      was tightly tied with rawhide thongs
      like a drum.

Now I am more loosely fitted,
      my edges even,
      more rounded and smoothed,
      gentler like a glacial pebble.

In the Middle East I carved my portrait
      in a green stone in Yemen.
      It was the Arabic word for cloud.

I am closer now to that cloud sculpture.
I am feeling my shadow more clearly,
      and if I do create another self-portrait,
      it will be drawn

in the sand on some warm beach
as the tide comes in,
so it can be erased,
and I can walk away from it,
smiling.

September 1998
Santa Fe, New Mexico
Published 2002: Poetry Contest Winner: *Passager*,
Mary Azrael and Kendra Kopelke, editors

At the Edgelessness of Light
—in memory of Paulette Beall

I have spoken enough of darkness:
    early years playing hopscotch
    with a single piece of broken glass
    without a playmate, playing
    hide-and-seek
    with a growing crowd of sharp-eyed ravens.

With a room full of paint and brushes,
    ink and canvas, stone and chisels,
    I built mountains close enough to the sky
    that I could throw new stars
    into constellations others named
    "Coming Home" and "Maps to the Future."

As the darkness filled more and more
    with clues to how things happen,
    winters became shorter,
    shadows thinner,
    harsh words softer,
    and chinks in the wall became
    undulating crosshatches of edgeless light.

Sorry. I began to speak to you about light.

It is just that I wanted you to know
    about the remnants of darkness first,
    before I go blind
    and the moon sucks me up.

        17 July 2003
        Santa Fe, New Mexico

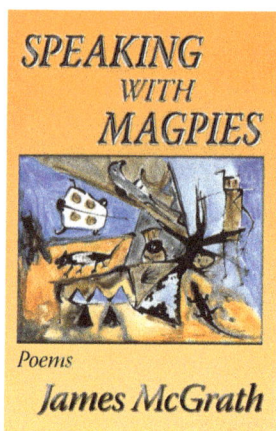

SPEAKING
WITH
MAGPIES

Poems

James McGrath

Speaking With Magpies, 2007
Selections by Cynthia West

These poems raised their hands to be selected because of the power with which they convey James' deepest cares and sorrows. Rooted in the Irish bardic tradition, they emit a pure stream of poetry that connects us to ancient truths. Clear, direct nature images, sometimes spiced with whimsy, articulate his main themes, love and loss of family, friends and relationships. Another recurring subject is anger over injustice and cruelty, not only to humans but also to all life forms. He unearths the gifts to be won from darkness and suffering. His masterful expressions of grief open us to acceptance of our own pain, while enhancing the understanding that we are not alone but a vital part of nature's totality.

Writing with James over the last twenty years has been a source of pure inspiration. Significance that seldom needs revision flows from his pen. After teaching thousands, over much of the planet, for a grand number of decades, his deep listening continues to bring words to life.

Some years, we wrote in groups. Other years, we worked in each other's homes, gardens and orchards. During visits to his house, the old stage coach stop in La Cieneguilla, he gifted me with some knowledge of Japanese Tea Ceremony. We served each other tea to create the quiet mind and heart essential for deep diving into the poetry ocean.

Currently, meeting weekly via telephone, we continue to surface with treasure. As earth-based humans, we praise the mountains, clouds, trees, plants and creatures.

Cynthia West is the author of six collections of poetry: *For Beauty Way*, 1990, and *1000 Stone Buddhas*, 1993, published by Inked Wingbeat, Santa Fe; *Rainbringer*, 2004, *The New Sun*, 2007, *In the Center of the Field*, 2010, *A Clear Drop*, 2015, and *Seed Keepers*, 2022, the last five published by Sunstone Press, Santa Fe.

In the Time of Drought
—for my friend Stewart Udall in memory of Lee

After the lake I drink from dries up,
      I will make the lake bed my home
      until the rains come again.

I will gather obsidian points
      in the ancestral wallows.

Dust-filled bird bones
      for making flutes
      will wail songs of water.

At dusk I will sit in silence,
      waiting for migrating geese
      to hover over the dryness.
      I will have only a single thermos
      of water to share with them.

How long can they stay with me?

I shall play my bird-bone flute for them.
      They will gather around me
      in concentric circles.

They will murmur of lakes filled
      with clouds, sing of lost trails
      and ancient resting places,
      where only cities grow.

They will describe rivers flowing
      with watercress, ponds of duckweed
      and reeds.

And when they leave at dawn,
      I will fly with them.

6 March 2004

There is a Magpie Inside Me
—*for my daughter Jeni Keleen Viney*

There is a magpie inside me
      next to the turtle and the dragonfly.

It speaks at odd hours.
      At night it awakens my dreaming foxes.

It flies to far-off places,
      holding clouds tight
      among its feathers,
      its beak carrying juniper berries.

It builds its nest in Spring
      before all snow melts.
      It listens to the seeping sounds
      of Winter weeping.

There is a magpie inside me
      next to the horse
      and the pterodactyl.

It waits, expecting hummingbirds
      to share their honey.

It preens its wings,
      making shining mirrors
      for iridescent beetles
      and star-eyed gnats.

It never sleeps.

It carries the sun from one horizon
      to the other.

It presses its head to my chest, it sings
      of loneliness and wild iris.

            12 September 2005
            Galisteo, New Mexico

We Were Two Crossword Puzzles

No need to ask if there was a double life
        between us.

It's what we got used to,
        creating habits to start the day
        after the darkness:
        the nice things we said
        to keep the hours open,
        the careful actions,
        testing the waters for directions.

We didn't want to startle ourselves
        or open cracks to fall into.

We didn't want to nail a secret
        on the wall of the bedroom so it bled.

I think we wanted to leave crumbs
        from the warm bread we broke at first.

We had hoped the crumbs might be
        the yeast for bigger, better loaves
        to share when it began to get dark
        and there were no constellations to read.

We came to one another with our double lives.

        Perhaps we expected them to merge,
        to be put together into a completed
        crossword puzzle that would be our map
        to who we really were.

As time went on, we discovered
    there were two crossword puzzles,
    not just one,
    and we had squares to fill in by ourselves,
    squares that had no clues to the answers.

Today when I open the box
    where I keep my crossword puzzle,
    I find some of the answers
    in those squares have changed.

    Some answers have faded beyond recognition.
    Some are polished and shining.
    Some are eyes that have closed,
    tired from staring too long.

    September 2004

It Carries Us Lightly
—for Aunt Margaret and Uncle Joe

What landscape blooms under the blue sky
      of my eyes?

Let me paint a picture for you.

I can see through wind-torn trees,
      around corners of roofless stone houses,
      into doorways without doors.
      White lichens are the lace curtains now.

Walk the Irish land with me, stepping
      over sparks of pink heather,
      nettles nibbling our ankles.

We will sit on limestone horses,
      peel bitter-scented bark
      from hazel walking sticks.

When we come to small gray cairns,
      we will find empty snail shells
      and black and white paintings
      in raven droppings.

A lark will be hovering, keeping her distance,
      drawing our eyes up to where she calls
      to rabbits and ghosts of potato farmers.

It is a land that harbors sadness,
      unafraid to cry or to feel lost,
      a land of hungry grasses
      that twist and flutter at my sighing.

It is a land where the names on the gravestones
        of our ancestors hold light,
        where empty roadsides bloom
        with red tears of fuchsia,
        where salty winds fill our ears
        with the sounds of tin pipes
        and the tight strings of fiddles.

When we walk on this land together,
        it carries us lightly,
        as if we belong here
        as if we have been here before.

        7 February 2004

The Grand Tour
—for my poet friend Judith Toler

My road has stones and potholes.

It branches off into grass, horsetails,
    mullein and a plot of wild roses,
    where birds nest in the Spring.

Just beyond, to the right,
    is a grove of early-blooming plums,
    edging a broken fence and an orchard,
    where poets read in good weather.

Leroy ropes an orange gate to a post
    to keep two face-nuzzling horses
    in the four-acre field, where they run
    from the gate to the river.

A hazel-wood memory of willows borders
    the river. Unnamed plants thrive
    in the undergrowth. Mysterious trails
    press down any grasses. Strong branches
    snatch at my sleeves when I walk by.

The river's edge eats and gurgles
    at a bare-rooted cottonwood that shares
    its map-meandering with a blue heron.

Footprints of deer mark gravel bars at the bend
    of the river.
    Raccoons have made bowls in sand-pockets
    for resting.

If I begin early in the morning,
   I can reach the river before the moon rises.

After I return home, I will write a poem.

   12 October 2005

The Hand on My Shoulder

What is left of the day
         as night fills this place
         is memory,
         laughter,
         a glass of wine
         and a candle.

What is left of the day
         as night calls the shapes of the moon
         and fits stars into blackness
         is the ravishing of daylight,
         the stealing of the scent of lavender,
         the giving away of songs
         birds have left behind.

What night brings
         is the unseen voices in the dust,
         the merging of dreams,
         the flutter of lost morning sighs.

What night brings
         is the blankness of unsaid words,
         the open space of walking alone,
         the hand on my shoulder
         and the kiss on my lips
         when you said goodnight
         for the last time.

                11 July 2004

Blue of Baghdad

When the smoke clears in Baghdad,
      will people in the streets
      hold their faces up to a blue sky?

If I were there,
      I would color the world blue:
      melt my crayons,
      smear them across the stones
      where blood has dried.

I would prepare blue paint,
      pressing blue from my jeans and shirts,
      unravel and soak indigo threads
      from rugs covering empty water jars.

I would dye my *galabiyya* blue,
      as if woven from the ancient free-flowing Euphrates.

I would dress my children in blue,
      the blue of their bruises,
      blue from the fallen roof of their home.

I would paint images of blue butterflies
      on the stones around our garden.
      Perhaps the foreign soldiers
      would not target them
      when they pass by.

          11 September 2005

To Celebrate the Dark
   —for my poet friend Marie Leontine Tsibinda

I celebrate the dark
        after it has passed.
        I see clearly what has
        bumped against me,
        thumped against my chest,
        pulled wax from my ears,
        stolen words from my poems,
        replaced them with hopeful images.

After it has passed
        I recognize the gate has always been open,
        the pathway always without end,
        and the stumbling was because
        I blinded myself.

I had left my rucksack open,
        thinking I wanted the moths to fly away,
        thinking that if I let the dark
        into all the pockets,
        pulled the zipper tight,
        I would have captured it,
        made it the prisoner
        it had made of me.

After it has passed
        I celebrate the dark.
        I praise those early morning hours
        when the moon flowed West,
        erasing the stars.

In my blood
      I know the darkness will come again
      to close the door for a brief time,
      but I will have the words and colors
      to paint my home
      in sweeping strokes of fire and water.

        8 August 2004

The Longest Winter

Here was a place to sit, wait, watch,
    to think thoughts but not to voice them.

The world was crowded with moons,
    one in each mud puddle.

He had longed for a visitor,
    anyone, to open his book,
    test verbs, modify nouns.

This was the longest Winter.
    Voiceless thoughts bound his feet in fog.

He ran out of paper,
    etched incomplete sentences
    in the soft plaster of his walls.

He carved words on garden stones,
    words magpies stole when his back was turned.

Wild rabbits and foxes left notes to him
    in their tracks on clotted mud,
    which he deciphered in the morning.

At night when moon-filled puddles shimmered
    with the cold, he laid his blanket over them,
    blinding the moon.

He preferred the dark where the sounds
    of the earth breathing sang the truth
    and gave him life.

23 March 2005

He Died Before I Could Hold Him

How many times did we say good-bye?

He enters my heart where all the silence
      is filled with his lonely wildness.

I hear his rippled laughter
      when he ran cold, shivering from the river.

He interrupts every song
      that summer colors leave behind
      in the morning garden.

There is no room for us
      in the bells of tulips.

He was all the music I needed to breathe.

I hear him snapping his brightness
      in the blazing fireplace.
      He leaves whispers in the ashes.

He colors every room
      in the memory-blue
      of holding hands
      between the pages of poetry.

If I sit long enough,
      the sounds that scuff across the floor
      vanish into fog that being too young
      sighs along the ground.

Now he arrives when the moon rises.

He carries it in his arms
when he knocks on my door.

How many times did we say good-bye?

There are questions that migrating birds
ask when they are lost.

There are voices like mine
that sit in trees
just before the saw cuts them down.

7 February 2006

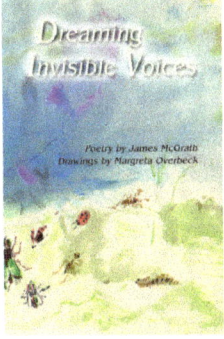

Dreaming Invisible Voices, 2009
Selections by David Cloutier

Written from a place of wonder, these poems are rare affirmations. On full display is James McGrath's acute sensitivity toward the natural world. There is a deep sense of abiding, dwelling on the earth, and a sweetness in his celebrations of the beings who inhabit his world. He gives voice to the plethora of unique creatures and to the elemental, natural forces that uphold them.

As in Native American and Asian expressions, McGrath captures his subject whole, through strong but simple utterances like *sumi* brush strokes. Complementing the poems are drawings by his friend and student Margareta Overbeck. Poet James and artist Margareta clearly tickled each others' fancies. The poems and drawings tumble page by page like children in the sun.

This collection could have been written for children, but in actuality, it addresses the inner child, from an inner child, to the inner child in all of us.

David Cloutier grew up in New England. He pursued creative and cultural studies at Goddard College and Brown University. He has worked as a teacher, literary publisher, arts council director, and festival producer in California, New Mexico, North Carolina and Rhode Island. Notably, he was the founder and director of the Monterey World Music Festival (1997-2003), one of the few North American festivals devoted to world music. His books of poems include *Ghost Call*, *Tongue and Thunder*, *Soft Lightnings*, and *Bird Conjuring*. He has translated books of contemporary French poets Jean Laude and Claude Esteban, and has published several volumes of versions from the oral poetry world, including *Spirit Spirit: Shaman Songs*. He lives in Santa Fe, New Mexico.

To the Human

You are the human.

Each and every space
        between the breathings of time
        is a mirror for you,

        a bright window to examine, polish,
        shatter, to love what you see.

It is time for you to share
        the light that enters your soul.

That is your reflection.

Bee

Perhaps
> my life is as blessed
> as yours.

I keep the flowers alive.

I help fruit sweeten the world.

I create the most succulent
> food on earth.

When I work, I waggle-dance and sing.

Perhaps
> my life is as blessed
> as yours.

You receive the scent of flowers.

You have the sweetness of fruit.

You eat the gold of honey
> and when you work in joy
> you can create songs and dances.

Perhaps
> you and I are both blessed.

Bird
—in memory of my flicker *Flicka*

The clouds are my family.

When you cannot find me,
      it is because my sisters
      and brothers have called me.

We are singing circles of prayers
      about the earth.

I shall build a nest for you
      to rest in.

It will be soft and half-round
      like the moon in your spirit.

Please come to the nest
      I build for you.

It is made of woven loves
      and is lined with feathers
      of plum and cherry.

Caterpillar

Like you, I must change.

As much as I love wandering
      among petunias and apple blossoms,
      my roaming years are brief.

Unlike you, I know I will change
      into something beautiful
      though short-lived.

When you see me dreaming in a rose,
      remember beauty begins with wandering
      and is short-lived.

Four Seasons

Spring sees you awakening,
        beginning songs
        for breaking shells
        with larks and nightingales
        and moves on.

Summer scents your body
        in your spiciness,
        your roseness,
        your marigoldness
        and moves on.

Autumn pauses, listens to you
        shaking and storing
        bits of your life for replanting
        and moves on.

Winter watches you capturing
        shadows in gardens
        of sand and stone
        and moves on.

Frog

We will hop and jump and plop
    and splash
    from early Spring into Summer
    and late Autumn, then go
    hopping and jumping and plopping
    and splashing
    into Winter
    when we will pause and rest
    and sleep with seeds.

There we will build new vigor
    for ourselves
    and for the world.

We will wait for the next Spring
    when the first rain
    will call us awake.

Then we will hop and jump and plop
    and splash
    from early Spring into Summer
    and late Autumn, then go
    hopping and jumping and plopping
    and splashing
    into Winter
    when we will pause and rest
    and sleep with seeds.

Mountain

If you watch the moon rise
> over my peaks and valleys,
> you will know that the moon
> is my gift to you.

Even if you are at sea,
> somewhere the moon
> has come up over a mountain
> to give its light to your path.

I will never hold the moon
> in my arms for long.

You must have its changing brightness
> for the darkness in your life.

Plant

Life and death.

Blooming, harvested, lying dormant.

Flowers and seeds
        are gifts
        of my cycle.

They are all good. I have learned
        to let them pass by,
        accepting each in their time.

I let them pass
        so that I may survive
        and grow, and grow.

Rain

When I float across the sky,
    over the earth and oceans
    softly, hanging like a veil
    or a skein of long hair,
    I am the she-rain.
    I am fertility.

When I rush over the mountains,
    the deserts, along wave tips,
    bringing lightning, thunder,
    heavy clouds, and pounding the earth,
    I am the he-rain.
    I am fertility.

I give this fruitfulness to you,
    the gentleness of she-rain,
    the firmness of he-rain.

You must have both to be human.

Each is your strength.

Each is your weakness.

Spider

Have you seen my web in moonlight,
      circle upon circle upon circle
      of brightness?

Have you seen my web in sunlight,
      illuminated circles upon circles?

In the mornings when there is dew
      in the air, I weave upon the edges
      of crystals.

Start at the center of my woven labyrinth,
      use my threads to weave
      yourself a swallowtail of light,
      beginning here and ending there.

This will be your spirit garment
      so you may move in beauty
      where flowers bloom,
      where waters flow,
      where stones are still.

In the night, when there is prayer
      in the air, we will weave together
      on the edge of a star.

Wind

Sit with me.
     Let me surround you.

I shall carry your cries and murmurs
     to become your voice
     for a thousand years.

I shall speak for you
     through masks of beaten gold,
     masks of carved wood and bone,
     masks covered with painted cloth.

I shall travel about the universe,
     entering pyramids and tipis,
     caves, openings behind stars
     and rusted bodies of ships.

I shall travel out of time.

I shall meet you on your return journey
     on your way home.

We shall talk together to awaken sleeping shadows
     in the dusty mirrors.

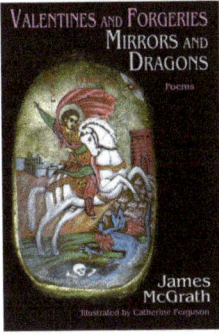

Valentines and Forgeries, Mirrors and Dragons, 2011
Selections by Ann Yeomans

James McGrath has a continuous ability to be open to life, to new experiences, to sensuality and to deepening his contact with inner and outer worlds. He's always learning, and he often learns like a child, full of wonder and curiosity. You experience that in his poems. They tune your senses and your imagination to new ways of seeing and being. Within the poems, I'm able to feel when the iron bursts into flame, when the sword has pierced my heart, when I get acquainted with the dragon.

James' poems are an invitation, similar to the night he invited a friend and I for dinner. He'd grown a magnificent pumpkin squash and wanted to share it with us. We came to his elegant dining room table, laid with 18th century Japanese platters, and served us a scrumptious Argentinian stew with mouth watering chicken, peaches, corn, wondrous seasonings, all cooked up in this grand pumpkin. After dinner he said, "Let me read a poem I wrote after reading Lorca's essay on the *duende*." I tell you this because the way he prepared and offered dinner is very much the way he offers a poem. It's a feast!

The poem he read to us that night is "The Edge," one of the ten selected. In each poem you'll find succulent images to tease the daimons of your nature. Enjoy your meal!

Ann Yeomans has been an Archetypal Therapist and Creative Consultant for 30 years, entering into a dialogue with often unsettling experiences of life and dream. She works primarily with artists and writers like James to deepen a sense of soul through dreamwork, active imagination, sandplay, depth exploration and creative regeneration, entertaining and inviting the psyche in myriad ways. James has participated in many of these offerings, bringing his unique way of dancing with images and dreams to share with others.

To Write is to Love Again

When a poet writes of things hidden
    under stones or in dreams
    only nightmares leave behind,
    I implore them to plunge me deeper.

Sometimes a poet hints
    at the brownness of the horse.
    I want to inhale the sweat,
    to be stomped on by its hooves.

I want to be buried, memorialized
    in autumn leaves, then massaged away
    into a September orchard
    of ripe peaches being harassed by bees.

When a poet writes to the edge of the abyss,
    stops, turns around, waits,
    I want to be pushed over,
    to tumble and bounce against the stones,
    as I fall. If I do not reach the bottom
    in one piece, I can forgive the poet.
    I only want the terror of being torn open
    by a torrent of words.

I don't want a poet to boil me in a pot of stew
    leaving out the spices and the moment
    the heat is turned down forgetting
    the scorching and the burning.

I want my ears to be seared
    by the memory of abandoned love,

my eyes to flame when I read
of the emptiness that turns tears into steam.

And if I could write a poem like the stars fall,
I would read to you tonight
and be rekindled into a wildfire.

6 October 2006
Santa Fe, New Mexico

The Real Thing

There is that open space
    between the trees in my orchard,
    where grass is short,
    the boughs low,
    the sky drops around me when I hold my arms open.

This is where the path spreads out,
    one side wild plum,
    three sides apple.

This is where people have gathered
    to read poems, to celebrate
    birthdays, weddings,
    to share foods, fruits,
    to embrace one another.

This is where one hundred women
    could lie face down together,
    becoming mothers of earth again,
    where one hundred men
    could sit back-to-back together,
    feeling one another's spine,
    sharing the softness of their bodies again.

This is a sacred place, where I walk in circles,
    humming like a bee calling out my name,
    speaking with ancestors
    on my tongue,
    listening to the silence that can never be filled.

This is where the wind is breathing,
   asking for nothing,
   where the earth waits
   to be loved over and over again.

5 February 2009
Santa Fe, New Mexico
Published in *New Mexico Poetry Review,*
Spring 2010

•

A Meeting in Yemen in a Time of Flood

We stood together alone on the bridge into town,
    only because she had fallen against me
      when the wall of water hit the bridge we were standing on.

She clung to my shoulders in the sweep of water
    swirling down the river bed at the West Gate
      to the Old City.

Her burkha was entangled, twisted about us,
    her scarf and veil torn from her head,
      her stream of hair the color of mud.

The kohl about her eyes ran in black rivulets
    down her cheeks.

She was shaking. I was shaking.

min faDlak, law samaHt.

Excuse me, please. *min faDlak, law samaHt.*

That was all we could shiver in conversation,

I could tell from her face, her eyes wide, sad,
    crying, that she was apologizing for the river,
      the water, the mud, our entanglement, our debris.

We stood there in the hot sun, in the whispering
    flood waters.

In the corner of her burkha she had tied a flat loaf
    of bread. Miraculously, she unwrapped the bread
    with her pomegranate-tattooed fingers.

She fed me a bit of crust. It had a pocket
    of Taiz honey that burst and ran down my chin.

She laughed, fingered off the honey, offered
    her sweetened fingertips to my tongue.

I laughed. Mud was drying on our legs and arms.
    The water receded with sweet bread crumbs
    floating to the south where the river ran away
    with our secret.

January 1993
Sana a, Yemen

A Walk in the Jungle

When I left the museum,
    I continued drawing, counting
    the black birds in the wheat field.

They erupted from the frame, plucking out my eyes
    until everywhere there was blackness
    and the scalding heat
    of "You're not good enough!"

When I left the lecture room,
    I continued writing, pouring
    line after line of watery adjectives
    on the burning fire.

The words burned holes in the arms
    of my winter coat
    until, armless, I called
    for a wheelchair and a large pink eraser.

But those days were before
    the apricot blossoms
    made light-filled pools
    on my table.

Now when I hold a raindrop
    up to my lips, I can taste
    the beginnings of conversations
    between the mountain and the moon.

It was only when I knew my name
    was not my name
    that I could speak into the ears of tigers.

23 March 2007
Santa Fe, New Mexico

Leave-taking

Before I leave
    I want to stand naked,
    hidden inside my skin,
    next to the model
    in Michelangelo's studio.

I want to hear the fall of marble chips
    on the floor.

I want to feel the sculptor's eyes
    caressing the neck of the model,
    to feel his fingers molding
    the chest and the genitals.

I want to stand naked
    next to that model,
    to taste the heat
    in the strength of shoulders,
    the firmness of flesh in stone.

I want to see tears from the sculptor's
    eyes become the sparks from his chisel.

Is there silence between the hammer
    and the chisel, or is there
    an angel singing in the blossoms
    outside the studio window?

Does the floor tilt toward
    where I sit with the model?

Will we roll together into the sculptor's arms
  when the figure is finished?

There is no breathing of dust
  in this studio.

There is only the sound of breath
  from the piercing arrows
  of the sculptor's eyes
  as he carves away the excess stone
  to free what he loves.

And when it is over and he leaves
  his studio, I will dress the model
  in my clothes, gather the fallen chips
  from the floor to eat them
  as my heart eats the days
  I have left to live.

30 March 2009
Galisteo, New Mexico

Tiepolo's Ceiling
  —for Jennifer Carrasco, artist-friend

Tiepolo had sad dreams of Icarus
        when he was four.

He thought his pillow was a cloud.

He thought his mother's billowing apron
        a cloud, his father's pantaloons clouds.

At five, Tiepolo saved jars of soapy water;
        he would shake them, making clouds
        for his aunts and uncles.

His school-friends thought him crazy.

At six, he was the first to waken
        to climb onto the roof,
        to drink the clouds.

He was intoxicated with clouds at seven.

By the time he was eight, he told his tutors
        his name was Cumulus, signed his letters
        Cumulus.

His father was not happy with his change of name.

One Friday at the age of ten, he locked
        the door to his room, painted his ceiling
        with pink, white, orange clouds,
        made a self-portrait peering out
        of a blue-eyed sky.

His father was bewildered.

It was only when Tiepolo painted the ceiling
of the Church of the Gesuati in Venice,
a cosmos of clouds, angels, cherubs,
blue-eyed sky did his father rejoice in
his reaching for heaven.

Today, the clouds over the Sangre de Cristo
Mountains flow East all summer.

They come to Venice to join the angels
and cherubs.

Tonight when Tiepolo floats across the ceiling
of my room, I will dream I am a cloud.

8 August 2008
Galisteo, New Mexico

The Homeless Man

He left the city,
    carrying holes of childhood in his pockets.

His fingers looped through his belt.

He walked just above the earth,
    leaving no footprints.

The roadway rustled autumn.

Crickets emerged from under stones,
    singing when he passed.

His face, a neon of loneliness,
    his hair tangled with moths,
    eyes the leaves from a book
    of endangered birds.

I saw his arms holding emptiness,
    bruised blue.

His back straight, where bees
    had built a winter hive.

The sound of wind rushed
    through the harp of his ribs.

Statues on the cathedral watched
    his shadow pass by, waved their wings,
    tears running down their stone cheeks.

23 October 2008
Santa Fe, New Mexico

The Sound of an Echo

No one can explain the night
    to dogs and widows.

What is lost becomes a menagerie
    of bones and wedding rings.

On the path up the hill
    stones open their wings
    to let dragons slip by.

Songs are etched on broken eggshells,
    hiding in abandoned nests of robins.

Somewhere dawn rises in fields of raspberries
    that magpies press, preening their feathers.

If I call her name from across the lake,
    waves appear in the shape of lips.

Nothing has a softer kiss than the foam
    at the edge of water.

Perhaps the breathing of turtles
    is the sound of an echo.

Perhaps it is in the opening of hands
    we see the words given to us
    by our mother before we were born.

Nothing is heard when the moon
    vanishes over the mountain in the West.

If I live long enough,
    I will give my skin to a coyote.

6 July 2007
Santa Fe, New Mexico

My Winter Soldier

My brother played drums in his high school band.

He sang Bacharach songs to Fatima down the road.

He tickled my mother with a peacock feather.

He laughed at my 4th grade elephant jokes.

He teased Dad about his bright ties.

My brother came home last week from Iraq.

He wore a piece of shrapnel from his shoulder
    on a chain around his neck.

He had a prosthetic arm with five plastic fingers
    in a white glove.

He called Dad a motherfucker because he wore
    a tie.

He said he had shot elephants and peacocks
    in the Baghdad zoo for target practice
    with his buddies.

He said Fatima was just another stupid Hajji.

He sold his drums on e-bay.

Last night at dinner he told us how they poured
    gasoline on a library in Fallujah, shooting

into the shadows until they ran red.

How the books burned; even Rumi couldn't escape
      the flames.

He cried in his room all night, tossed grenades
      of four-letter words into the dark.

This morning he never came down to breakfast.

18 March 2008
Santa Fe, New Mexico
Published in *Against Agamemnon: War Poetry,* 2009
Published in *Sin Fronteras: Writers Without Borders,* 2007

The Edge

Let me tell you about the edge.

To know the edge
    is to live at its brow, at the border,
    a horizon on one side,
    a chasm on the other side.

No beginning and no end,
    except when I stutter.

To live on the edge
    is to be possessed in darkness
    with a single keyhole of light
    for breathing. Here is where
    walls are looking for color.

There is sharpness here,
    the sharpness of gasping for air,
    for taking in bird feathers,
    broken trees, the scent of cedar.

And dullness, the dullness of jumping
    into a valley of fog
    that wild animals have abandoned.

This is where I stomp on the grapes of blindness.

This is the lonely place.
    I come here to be alone,
    leaving my shadow behind,
    nailed on a fence post.

This is the place where a poet destroys words
        to find new meanings for darkness and light,
        the place where feelings are sandstorms
        and typhoons, where I take off my shirt
        from too much sweating, a place where
        I taste my salt.

It is the trap I never abandon
        so I can find my way home.

This is where I find it most easy
        to love and to be loved in the hollowness.

There is no map, no signboard.

The edge has no name when it is discovered.

It's like digging a ditch with a spoon
        to bury the rainbow. What is left
        is the sharp pain of something
        lost I never had.

This is the place I cut open my chest
        to give my heart to what loves me.

        23 October 2009
        Santa Fe, New Mexico

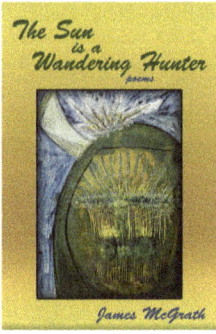

The Sun Is A Wandering Hunter, 2015
Selections by Verma Nequatewa and Robert Rhodes

James has a way of saying things in poetry that resonates with Hopi. He understands the place, the spirit, the feelings of Hopi and transforms that into words that enable us to say "Yes…. that is how it is." James uses words in ways that most of us don't think of. For example, "This is What Dreams Me" makes perfect sense, but who else would have thought of wording it that way. And "Rain in Five Parts" says just enough and captures the feelings perfectly. "I Sing With My Fingers" understands the relationship between the artist, the stones, and the place. James sees and expresses how the world and the animals in it are and relate to each other and how blessed we are to be able to witness it. Through his poetry he elevates his experiences so that the rest of us can see.

Verma Nequatewa knew and knows James through her uncle, Charles Loloma. James and Charles worked together at the Institute of American Indian Arts. Then James invited Charles to be Artist-in-Residence in Japan, Korea, and the Philippines. James visited Charles, Verma and Hopi many times, often witnessing Hopi ceremonies. They all worked together on the filming of the PBS documentary, "Loloma." James worked with Robert Rhodes and visited Charles and Verma during two visits as Artist-in-Residence at Hotevilla-Bacavi Community School. He stayed with Verma and Bob later as an instructor for Hopitutuqaiki, The Hopi School, when Bob was the facilitator. Both Bob and Verma think of James as a mentor who lives and breathes art.

James adds: Three poems, "I Sing With My Fingers," "This Is What Dreams Me," and "Here Is The Turquoise Song," are from *Visions of Sonwai: Verma Nequatewa*, by Annie Osburn, the pictorial, biographical book about Verma, the internationally renowned Hopi jeweler from Hotevilla, Arizona, the Hopi reservation.

After a Night of Wind

After a night of wind from the moon,
    I follow the dawn tracks of animals
    crossing the road.

I make human footprints
    that raise dust
tempting beetles
    to lose their way.

The silence under a July cedar tree
    holds tight to shadows.

Nothing moves except the anguish
    of an ant caught
    in the sweet honey of tree sap.

Yesterday a brown stone lay burnishing
    in the dust. This morning it was gone,
    encased in sand that had danced
    all night making drum beats
    with its family of smallest stones.

This is the land where spirit lives.

The body will wither,
    shake like dried corn stalks.

The spirit remains touched by clouds
    waiting to sing,
    waiting to be heard.

      16 July 2006
      Hotevilla, Hopi Reservation, Arizona

They Say My Name is Corn

They say my name is corn.

They say I walked for centuries
    searching for home.

They say my path from the South
    gave me red,
    Paalangpu. *

They say my path from the West
    gave me yellow,
    Sekyangpu. *

They say my path from the North
    gave me blue,
    Sakwa. *

They say my path from the East
    gave me white,
    Qotsa. *

They say your land
    gave me life.

They say your song
    gave me life.

They say your dance
    gave me life.

They say your prayer
    gave me life.

They say I grow strong in soil called home.
    My name is corn.
    My name is home.

    27 July 2011
    Hotevilla, Hopi Reservation, Arizona

* Color words in the Hopi language.

Over Here, Over There

Where does the horizon begin?
I must turn my head to find it.

>   To the East clouds are resting.
>   To the South clouds are resting.
>   To the West clouds are resting.
>   To the North clouds are resting.
>   Here where I am sitting
>   I am resting.

Where does the horizon end?
I must turn my head to find it.

>   22 July 2009
>   Hotevilla, Hopi Reservation, Arizona

This is How I Walk

There are footprints in the sand
    that dance when the wind sings.

    This is how I walk.

There are trails between stones on the mesa
    left by foxes and coyotes.

    This is how I walk.

There are tracks on the branches
    of peach and juniper
    left by jays and bluebirds.

    This is how I walk.

There are pathways from yesterday to tomorrow
    left by ancestors.

    This is how I walk.
    This is how I walk home.

    15 July 2008
    Hotevilla, Hopi Reservation, Arizona

House of Blessings
—For Robert Rhodes and Verma Nequatewa, Hotevilla

In the morning
    when the gray fox, the yellow fox,
    the red fox have run from the sky
    to the East, I walk the path
    to the House of Blessings.

The Path through *Munsi Tsomo* is edged
    in *Sohu*, the rock rose, *Munsi*,
    the paint brush, *Hootski*, the juniper.

My footsteps are brothers to the night dog,
    the morning lizard and the shadows
    of speechless trees.

The *Paalangpu*, red, of *Munsi*, warms my walk.

The *Qotsa*, white of the rock rose, gives me
the white light of morning.

I can not count the thousand and thousand footsteps
    rain left in the dust last night.

Somewhere in the *Hootski* a mocking bird announces
    songs to the clouds and sleeping stones.

The path will remember me by the footsteps
    I have left in the sand on my way to
    the House of Blessings.

This is how I walk when the sun rises
      and the gray fox, the yellow fox,
        the red fox and I go home each morning.

      20 July 2011
      Hotevilla, Hopi Reservation, Arizona

Rain in Five Parts

I am asking for the rain.
It is coming.
It is here.
It has left.
Thank you.

20 July 2009
Hotevilla, Hopi Reservation, Arizona

In Rick's Field

I walked among corn
    dancing green this morning
    in Rick's field.

My first steps heavy
    leaving prints in the sand.

I walked among melons and gourds
    stretching their green arms this morning
    in Rick's field.

My ears listened for hints
    of rattle songs to come.

I walked among beans
    rustling their green leaves and tendrils
    this morning in Rick's field.

My tongue tasting
    the soft browning of future stews.

My eyes painted
    green corn tassels preparing
    for butterflies to dance
    among them.

My eyes painted
    a black beetle moving
    among corn, beans, gourds and melons
    humming its green song
    of beautiful mornings
    in Rick's field.

Stepping lightly
    leaving no footprints
    carrying growing green happiness
    that calms how I walk about the earth
    I left Rick's field.

    17 July 2014
    Hotevilla, Hopi Reservation, Arizona

One Long Poem

It is the repeating of silent rhythms
    that is dance and song
    the poem in this place.

It is the vision of earth colors
    red, orange, yellow, brown
    that is the poem in this place.

It is the small leaves of rock rose
    stipple pattern of cactus
    red tips of paint brush, *Munsi,*
    that is the poem in this place.

It is the open spaces between summer clouds
    breathing of summer winds
    rustle of junipers, *Ygapi,*
    that is the poem in this place.

It is the morning sun blessing
    wren song, mocking birds, doves
    that is the poem in this place.

It is the unseen architect building sand hills
    leaving space for fields to green
    that is the poem in this place.

It is the open land that invites you
    into its place fullness
    that welcomes you here,
    that makes you the poem in this place.

It is when you become the poem
    in this place that you know
    you are home.

    27 July 2014
    Hotevilla, Hopi Reservation, Arizona

From *Visions of Sonwai*

I Sing With My Fingers: A Foreword

My Uncle said,
    "I feel the stone and think,
    not to conquer it,
    but to help it express itself." (I)

My creating is like my cooking:
    singing blessings of corn,
    hearing bubblings of *Somiviki*,
    tasting *Nanagopsi* in the rabbit stew,
    smelling juniper and desert rose
    coming through the doorway from the East.

Kogyangsowuti, Spider Woman, dances above my head,
    She weaves her silver blossoms for me to sing to.

Kogyangsowuti rests with me.
    With her spirit eyes.
    She hums my fingers to create beauty.

I sing with my fingers.

Together, Spider Woman and I give thanks
    to Mother Earth and Father Sun.

And when I sit with the Sun in my studio,
    the stones wait for me in vibrating silence,
    the corn hums inlaid in its husk
    in colored drum beats.
    Visions of Sonwai burst open behind my eyes.

I sing with my fingers.

My bracelets and rings will be inlaid
    with turquoise and coral,
    corn from my Uncle's field
    where he sang to butterflies
    making love to squash blossoms.

My bracelets and rings will be inlaid
    with a sky of lapis lazuli,
    a blue that mountain birds
    leave behind when migrating South.

In the morning when I greet the Sun,
    the whiteness of my *Homa*, my cornmeal,
    is the half-moon that has fallen
    into my heart while I was sleeping.

It is only in the darkest night
    when stars whisper my name
    that I know my jewelry
    sings my song to you
    to make you more beautiful.

I sing with my fingers.

    (I) Charles Loloma, as quoted in *Arizona Highways*,
    "Charles Loloma," by Marjel De Lauer, August, 1976, p. 12.
    Somviki: cooked sweetened blue cornmeal
    Nanagopsi: a wild herb
    Homa: ground white cornmeal
    Kogyangsowuti: Spider Woman

    Santa Fe, New Mexico
    1 April 2007

    Visions of Sonwai: Verma Nequatewa, by Annie Osburn. Foreword.
2007.

This Is What Dreams Me

I sing the word Rain
     many times in one day.

I listen for thunder,
     inviting its voice into our fields,
     upon our homes, into our hands.

I sing the word Rain,
     listening to changing clouds.

I create images of clouds
     many times in a single day
     as our ancestors visit us.

Somewhere someone is singing.

This is what dreams me.

     Hotevilla, Hopi Reservation, Arizona
     16 July, 2006

     Visions of Sonwai: Verma Nequatewa, by Annie Osburn. p. 54.
2007.

Here Is The Turquoise Song

Here in my fingers is the turquoise song
  sung to me by my ancestors.

I cut and shape the words of the song
  into my bracelet.

I hum the high voice of coral

I hum the low voice of wood.

All about me are the moonlight rhythms
  of silver, the candlelight whiteness
  of ivory, the lapis blue of Winter sky.

When corn ripens,
  when *Kachinas* come to my village,
  when the *Piki* house hums,
  I drink a cup of *Hohoysi*.
  I think of gold for melting
  to create a rainbow around your wrist.

I hum the voice of *Joshposi*,
  the voice of turquoise.

All is beautiful.

   Piki: paper-thin, rolled, blue cornbread
   Hohoysi: wild herbal tea
   Joshposi: turquoise stone

   Santa Fe, New Mexico
   3 April, 2007

   Visions of Sonwai: Verma Nequatewa, by Annie Osburn. p. 84.
2007.

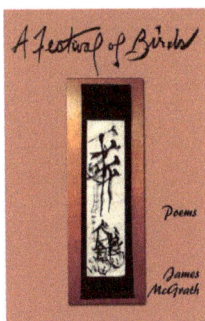

A Festival of Birds, 2017
Selections by Dale Harris

At the center of my love for haiku is a love of birds, especially Sandhill cranes. Because I live in the Rio Grande Valley, I witness their annual migration and mark the change of seasons by their coming and going. James McGrath shows that same love in *A Festival of Birds*. In the dedication, he says, "Love is the unnamed bird of Memory." This book is a primer for those of us who aspire to write haiku well. It is a demanding poetic form because it requires economy of words and agile use of metaphor. James McGrath stands tall among modern American poets who write in the spirit of haiku without the burden of mechanistic syllable counting and other conventions. A difference is that his aesthetic is so grounded in classical Japan that the poems read as though written centuries ago. Haiku at its best is simple and intense. These are love poems, passionate and direct despite their restraint. They are an invitation to remember our own hearts.

Dale Harris is an artist and poet living in Albuquerque's Sawmill Neighborhood. Her poems are widely anthologized and she enjoys performing at a variety of venues and arts festivals. Dale organizes the annual Poets Picnic at the City of Albuquerque Open Space Visitor Center, an event that features haiku submissions from New Mexico poets displayed on Weathergrams. Her book of haiku *Orchard Dreams* celebrates the fabled poetry readings at James McGrath's Apple Orchard in La Cieneguilla, New Mexico.

Let us write

    the names of the birds

    we hear

    hidden in the clouds

    to remember

    our names

I know you are near

when I find a feather

in the garden

I hold my poems

    as I hold my breath

    in a hibiscus

    where birds blush their songs

When I write my poems

    to you

    the rhythm

    is the bamboo whisk

    on the edge of a tea bowl

My loving you

    has happened before

    iris in *Meiji-jingu*

    stone images

    pausing late in *Ryoanji*

    this loving you

    is iris and stone

Meiji-jingu: a major shrine-temple in Tokyo noted for its iris garden.

Ryoanji: the quintessence of Zen art; the fifteenth century garden in Kyoto with fifteen stones.

Birds sing one song

"please remember me"

When I greet you

    in rare moments

    at the end of a day

    a gift of a thousand cranes

Each night

I walk the earth

in moonlight

your shadow next to me

I shall take the clay of memory

in my hands

fashion a tear bowl

to hold your passing

We lost time

    we lost one another

    before we started

    did you know it was too late

    to pick persimmons

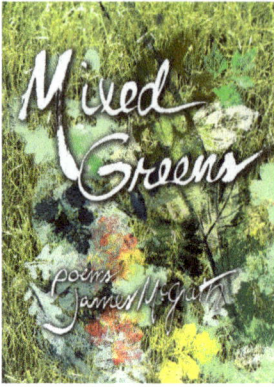

Mixed Greens, 2019
Selections by Catherine Ferguson

As I reread *Mixed Greens*, I stop after "Deafness in the Garden," struck by James' ability to write about the no-garden of winter, reminding me even in the cold silence there is a cat purring. In "The Soldier from the North Side" James' compassion reaches to anyone who is in pain or oppressed. With "The Moving Day," James shares his brown-bag lunch and wants to help. My eyes fall on "Snow," with its lovely sensuality. In "How We Touch," James invokes the "you," asking, "What have you done with your life?" "I Am Sorry" makes me laugh and cry. I like James' wondrous desire to get things done with no cell phone. James is not afraid to look in the shadows of childhood as he does in "Hide-and-Seek," wondering at the danger in thrown rocks. "10 January 2017" is a poem of praise to the world, a reminder not to intrude upon nature, not to "cut too many limbs from the fruit trees." James asks us to find a balance with the work we do as the robin does not exhaust itself singing, and the plover is never too tired to fly home.

Catherine Ferguson is a poet and painter who lives in Galisteo, New Mexico, where she walks with her dog. She met James years ago in a poetry class taught by Joan Logghe. For over twenty years Catherine has been writing with James, giving each other prompts, then reading aloud. In many ways Catherine shares James' view of the world. Catherine has won two New Mexico Book Awards: one for poetry as co-author of *The Sound a Raven Makes* and another for her retablo illustrations in *You Who Make the Sky Bend* by Lisa Sandlin. Catherine's poetry collection *I Thought You Would Be Shelter* was published by Sunstone Press in 2017.

Deafness In the Garden

How silent it is in the garden.

No whispering among sad-eyed asters.

No crossing of legs among iris.

No grinding of teeth from petals of marigolds.

No rattling in seed pods of poppies.

I only wanted to hear poems
  left alone
  with stones and broken twigs
  of my winter.

Now as I sit behind a wall
  of window glass
  joining the courtship of geraniums,
  I squint my eyes
  at the whiteness of the January sun,
  stretch my ears
  to hear the cat purring
  on the arm of the aging faded chair.

1 January 2013
La Cieneguilla, Santa Fe, New Mexico

The Soldier from the Southside

He spent his life celebrating nightmares,
    soundings of war,
        warning angels to stand back.

He argued with station masters who greeted
    strangers rolling about in snowbanks.

He shined hubcaps, throwing them across
    the wasteland where he fought over them
    with ravens.

He gave truth to the leaves that stole autumn
    before frost lied to them,
    shrouding his neighborhood.

There was an eerie trust cresting in his heart,
    waves that rolled ceaselessly in and out
    of his head.

I saw him for the last time driving an 18 wheeler
    headed for San Francisco, an American flag
    on his side aerial, a spare tire hanging loose
    where his rear view mirror should be.

I hear he never reached San Francisco.

His mother received a package at Christmas time
    postmarked Baghdad. Inside were her son's
    rearview mirror and the hubcaps from his trunk.

10 September 2010
La Cieneguilla, Santa Fe, New Mexico

The Moving Day

Lace up your shoes.

Tie up your scarf.

Close your brown-bag lunch.

Step into the mud
        on the road into town.

Forget to lock the door.

Leave the dead flies
        on the window sill.

This is the time to let
        your feet take you
        on your journey.

Leave your head home.

Let your heart walk you.

Along the road into town,
        pick up the beer cans,
        pick up McDonald's styrofoam cups,
        pick up the candy wrappers.

They will dissolve into nothing
        as you walk on the road into town.

You will think of the refugees
        at the fence:

those who weep,
those without food.

You are the refugee
        along your road into town:
        you are weeping,
        you are without food.

It's what you do
        when you forget
        to say thank you
        in the morning.

It's what you do
        when your heart's pen
        runs out of ink.

It's what you do
        before you cross the road into town
        to hold out your hand
        to the stranger on the other side,
        before you share your brown-bag lunch,
        before you tell them, I love you.

9 February 2017
La Cieneguilla, Santa Fe, New Mexico

Snow

You were on the mountain
        when the snow fell.

You let the snow flakes
        melt on your face.

You said,
        falling snow was the touch
        of my fingertips.

You said,
        melting snow was the touch
        of my lips.

14 March 2014
La Cieneguilla, Santa Fe, New Mexico

How We Touch

It is when we sat together on the granite boulder
        on the hillside of stones that you asked me
        what I have done with my life .

I waited until the clouds had passed
        and only the blue sky was on our shoulders
        to answer.

I waited until the footprints that had followed us
        filled with sprouting yarrow and verbena.

There was a long pause when I could breathe
        the sharp pollen from juniper, a pause
        that freed my breath.

Now I can answer with that same fertile pollen
        one yes-grain at a time:
        what I have done with my life. I hold it
        in my hand when we touch on that hillside
        of stones looking into the valley.

The lines in our palms will be the map
        to read to one another.

I will tell you how my path ends
        when the wind steals the last grain
        of pollen from my lips.

This is how we touch one another in the morning.

5 March 2012
La Cieneguilla, Santa Fe, New Mexico

I Am Sorry

No! I am sorry.
  I do not have email.

No! I am sorry.
  I do not have a cell phone.

No! I am sorry.
  I do not have a computer.

No! I am sorry.
  They do not deliver mail out here.
  I have a post office box in town.

Yes! Thank you.
  You can publish my poem,
  "This is my Life."

I love you.

27 January 2015
La Cieneguilla, Santa Fe, New Mexico

Hide-and-Seek

I wanted to cheat
    when we played hide-and-seek.

I wanted to see
    which way you went:
    into the garden or
    behind the house
    near the woodpile.

I could count to one hundred,
    turn,
    shake the dry cornstalks
    pretending I knew
    you were hiding there,
    dry as November corn.

    Turn,
    go behind the house.

    You were there
    in the woodpile,
    sculptured from the forest,
    smelling of cedar,
    fir and hemlock.

I could see the blue
    of your jeans huddled there
    among slivers and knots.

I was alone with you,

I never wanted to say I found you.

I wanted to hide with you.

Was I in danger
        finding you hiding in the shadows?

Would we leave the world together,
        leaving bread crumbs on our path
        in the woods?

I thought only cats and dogs
        knew danger:
        who threw the rocks,
        pulled the leash tight,
        built the fence too high
        to jump over?

A single stray cat
        comes to the back door now.

If I get too close
        it scatters off
        under the storage shed
        near my woodpile.

I leave food in the opening
        to its hiding place,
        make optimistic,
        hopeful sounds.

How long do I nurture that stray cat
        before it comes from hiding
        wanting me to share its warmth?

23 March 2015
Galisteo, New Mexico

Chopping Wood, Shoveling Snow

Now is the customary cold morning
        among faded morning glories
        and zinnias
        when the habitual wind
        and common birds
        knock on my kitchen door.

I need to open that door
        to see if anyone
        is chopping wood
        or shoveling snow.

It is early Winter.

Time to write those poems
        I have kept folded
        in brown paper bags
        since kindergarten.

I will title them Winter Poems,
        cold, dusty winter poems
        rustling with tootsie-roll wrappers
        and marbles.

This is when I will grab the axe
        to chop my own wood
        to fill the wood box.

This is how I will shovel snow
        from my path.

7 November 2016
La Cieneguilla, Santa Fe, New Mexico

Poem for My Daughter, JAIN

You put the fluff of a seagull breast feather
    into your hair.

Oh! How you chased it down the beach.

    How it rolled and erupted
    in the blowing echoes of wind.

    How it caught and struggled
    in the furze bush.

    How you gently lifted it
    into your hair from the thorns.

    How it stayed there fluttering
    and fluffing.

I thought you might fly away,
    that you might join the seagull
    crying alone on the rock
    where the waves pounded.

Now in my Winter years,
    I see that moment,
    the sea brightness in your eyes,
    the wind pushing and pulling
    our shadows into the surf.

    How the clouds of foam eddied
    around your feet.

    How you were lifted above the sand.

For a moment
    I thought I had lost you.

Now I only want to walk back
    to the clouds of foam,
    to follow our footsteps in the sand
    the sea of time has washed away.

I have taken the crying gulls
    into my heart.

7 January 2007
La Cieneguilla, Santa Fe, New Mexico

10 January 2017

We have not exhausted ourselves
    loving the world.

We have not dropped enough tears
    to fill the dried springs
    in the Galisteo Basin.

We have not kept enough dirt
    under our fingernails
    to welcome Spring.

We have felt the darkness
    crawling on our shoulders.

We have kept too much love
    under our tongues
    to name who loves us.

We have heard blood falling
    in our daily bowls of soup.

If we cut too many limbs
    from our fruit trees,
    birds can not find a place to sing.

We have not exhausted ourselves
    praising this world.

We have not gathered enough feathers
    for our wings.

We have not watched our footprints
    melting in the snow.

How many tea bowls have you made
    from the winter mud;
    how many blankets
    from the sunrise?

If we continually dig holes
    in our garden,
    morning glories and roses
    will not grow.

I have never heard of a robin
    too exhausted to sing;
    a plover too tired to fly home.

You may say, I am not a robin
    or a plover.

I am a refugee, like you.

10 January 2017
La Cieneguilla, Santa Fe, New Mexico

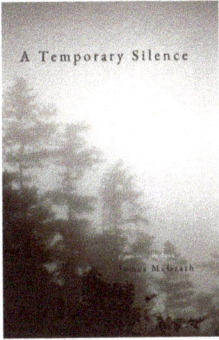

A Temporary Silence, 2021
    Selections by Paulette Frankl

"Old ghosts wait for us to knock
on any door of the hundreds
we keep closed. We do not need keys
or a secret password,
a memory will do."

—from "Old Ghosts Do Not Like Loneliness."

James' poetry speaks to a place so deep it makes me cry. I know this place. It is inside me as well. Nothing is unfamiliar here. I know that loneliness so absolute that we give it voice and names. We give it a background so as to make it comfy.

Just as my take away from Stanford was the ability to funnel the all-consuming immensity of an emotion into words that describe it and fit it onto a page so that others might experience that immensity from the juxtaposition of the words that create a size or volume or depth far bigger than the word or words themselves, so too does James' poetry take me on a slip-slide path both familiar but filled with surprises. I sense myself shape-shift to fit into his throbbing landscape so alive, gentle yet ferocious. Kindness becomes a gesture pierced with emotion: the hidden word uttered at last.

Paulette Frankl has been grappling with the immensity of expression both in words and in the imagery of art all her life. Born a Pisces into the combination of great aesthetic design in a time of war, her world has always been a dichotomy of opposites. Her insights come from her experiences of world travel and a life fully inhabited. She has published two books: *Lust for Justice: The Radical Life and Law of J. Tony Serra*, and *Marcel & Me*, about her 36 year liaison with the great mime Marcel Marceau. In Santa Fe her soul finds its home where she lives with the ghost of her magical cat, Sweetie, and a flock of ravens who consider her a member of their family.

Mirage

How I miss you
    when the invisible roots of you
    lie entangled with tulip bulbs
    and the view of snow falling.

This to say,
    you are the eternal journey
    I have taken
    without a map.

My dreams are the wanderers
    left in the hands
    of a stranger
    who walks with my shadow.

We step from stone to stone,
    from mountain to mountain,
    pausing to decipher
    the spiralling of pine cones
    that guide us the way
    through the forest.

Should we find ourselves
    in a canyon without an exit,
    let us lie down together
    to listen for the hoofbeats
    of ghost-horses. We will
    take their reins
    across the desert
    pausing long enough
    to be danced to exhaustion

by a lonely, distracted dust devil
I shall name, *mirage*.

21 August 2020
La Cieneguilla; Santa Fe, New Mexico

(Via telephone with Catherine Ferguson)

When I Leave

"...there is a likeness between dying and being somewhere that isn't here."
—Conor Cleary, "The American Wake,"
Still in the Dreaming: poems from Kerry 2017–2018.

When I leave,
    I will leave behind
    a narrow dirt road for you
    to match your footsteps
    with the ribbon-poem of the rattlesnake
    in the dust,
    and the minute etching
    of the feet of mice
    that disappear into the hole
    that was not there yesterday.

As I step over the shadows
    of fence posts lying
    in the road dust,
    there will be splinters
    from when I was told
    not to pick the apples
    before they ripened.

It was long ago.
    I stopped somewhere
    that isn't here.
    I saw my reflection
    in a store window
    where there were roller skates,
    red wagons,
    an orange tricycle

and a blue-black bicycle
for older boys:
mechanical things
for unnamed adventures
at the end of the road
that will be left behind
when I leave.

26 December 2018
La Cieneguilla; Santa Fe, New Mexico

We Are Loved In Our Memories

We are loved in our memories
    that stack one upon another
    in the darkness
    of the book without a cover.

Page after page
    of hopscotch
    and roller skates,
    brownies and butterscotch,
    haircuts and tears.

Chapter after chapter
    of butterscotch squares,
    of holding hands,
    kisses on the street corner,
    park benches.

Volume after volume
    of poems
    that blink
    and fly off the pages
    into the world of silence
    where they join
    winter clouds,
    images
    that change
    and color our dreams
    of how it was
    when we knew who loved us.

15 November 2019
Galisteo, New Mexico

The Right Moment To Fly Away

Can you name
        where you were before
        you were here?

This may be your birth place or
        where the bees left honey
        on your pillow.

No one should ask such questions
        of angels.

These are the questions
        limbs ask when they fall
        on a quiet day
        breaking the heart
        of a tree full of fruit.

A 4-leaf clover
        might give two
        of their 4-leaf answers
        before the moon rises.

There is a dog barking somewhere
        in the valley where fields of
        alfalfa are fenced in
        against coyotes.

This may be the place
        where gophers are safe,
        where raccoons can steal
        eggs of blue jays.

There is an opening in the clouds
     over the Sangre de Cristos
     where eagles fly.

This is the space
     where our shadows
     can leave us behind
     in the tops of pine trees.

When I have left my last shadow
     on the tallest pine branch,
     I will know the right moment to fly away.

26 June 2020
La Cieneguilla; Santa Fe, New Mexico

(Via telephone with Cynthia West)

Wearing The Mask Is Seeing In The Darkness

I walked the beach of a familiar island where seals left
    their skins on rocks with barnacles to swim naked
    with swirling flags of kelp.

    I stood still at the edge of a dead volcano expecting
    lichens to bloom yellow and orange painting a mask
    across my face.

    I waited for a whale to swallow the man who took my
    childhood but his breath had the smell of garlic.

    I sat in the park on the iron bench with the cast metal
    cherubs listening to their evening vespers
    in Latin expecting candles to burst into flames
    at the parking meters.

    I gathered chestnuts in the forest where Hansel and
    Gretel left candy wrappers for refugee children
    to find their way home before dark.

    I hid under a blanket of pine needles waiting for
    mushrooms and mint to put out the fires before
    the flames reached the mailbox.

    I left a final note in the nest of a robin with
    three blue eggs thinking the sadness of saying
    good-bye would be translated into Greek.

    I walked between the ages of ten and twenty as if
    the world had not begun, and if it rained,
    I could plant the seeds left behind by my father.

I opened the jar of peaches left in the back-seat
of the VW bus on a Sunday Morning in September,
thinking it was my birthday. Yellow jackets
flew out blinding me.

I write in the dark now.

Wearing the mask is seeing in the darkness.

19 September 2020
La Cieneguilla; Santa Fe, New Mexico

(Via telephone with Catherine Ferguson)

Living Another Year

This is the year
     the wild plums did not fruit
     and the milkweed did not send
     their yearly parachutes across the road.

This is an unruffled year
     among horsetails and willows.

Yet the road-dust still maps the deer
     coming into the garden
     and the cows in Tafoya's field
     remain begging at the fence.

Behind the mountain, the rainbow
     waits for the rain.

Clouds visibly become tired
     changing their shapes
     over-and-over even as winds
     tear them apart pulling rain clouds
     from thirsting desert gardens.

I think of the late summer days
     before school began,
     boys and girls waiting,
     changing from Tarzans and Janes
     into potential teacher's pets
     learning the names of patriotic heroes
     and the names of dogs that barked
     behind gates just before
     we got to the school yard.

I like waiting for a rain
    and thunder storm
    when the sun is shining,
    just before you remove your mask,

22 August 2020
La Cieneguilla; Santa Fe, New Mexico

(Via telephone with Catherine Ferguson)

The Way Home

There is a well-worn, creased,
        sweat-stained map we carry
        in our silence.

X marking the place, the people,
        the thing that changed
        our life.

We may polish the gold
        of who loved us,
        tarnished from neglect,
        so they outshine the new moon.

We may wipe the dust
        from the place we hid
        our dreams, muzzling
        the scarecrow of childhood.

We may replace the street sign
        to the market where the farmer
        of watercress sprinkled
        rain water on our heads,
        baptizing us, Nesting Bird.

The map remains in the pockets
        of our open hands for us
        to read when the darkness
        is too dark, when we ask
        for the light from the eyes
        of our beloved to see,
        and it is given to us.

The map we carry in silence
        has no North, no South,
        no East, no West.

The map we carry in silence
        is the way home.

11 March 2020
Santa Fe, New Mexico

This Time

Could it be
        this time,
        —this virus-time—
        is a childhood time for the artist,
        the poet we have kept alive
        waiting for the truth?

Those are not lies
        we kept close to pen and paper.

We just did not have the words then.

Now is the time
        —a virus-time—
        a time to put on a mask,
        to breathe from the heart.

Few listen to us.

They listen to their own heart beats,
        feel their own heat,
        taste their own blood.

The mesa is free to jump from.

The desert is open for running naked.

We can still skip rope
        and play hopscotch with bottle caps.

If we do not see the moon tonight
        before we sleep,

it is only because
we are looking somewhere else.

If our hands are cold in our dreams,
    it is only because
    we choose to sleep alone.

If we misspell words in our poems,
    it is only because
    we write so fast
    thinking there
    is so little time left.

No leaves are falling in the orchard.

25 May 2020
La Cieneguilla; Santa Fe, New Mexico

(Via telephone with Catherine Ferguson)

Old Ghosts Do Not Like Loneliness

We do not want
    to remember loneliness
    until we need
    echoes of sadness
    to keep us awake.

Old ghosts are a different thing,
    we welcome them or not.

Those old ghosts
    have a movable shrine
    of their own
    that may be on the pages
    of a book, or in the brief line
    of a song from childhood.

Old ghosts do not like loneliness,
    they prefer laughter.

Old ghosts wait for us to knock
    on any door of the hundreds
    we keep closed. We do not need keys
    or a secret password,
    a memory will do.

Old ghosts have the kindness
    of familiar strangers who remain
    waiting for us just around
    the corner.

Should a lonely old ghost appear
    uninvited, perhaps they are only

asking to be touched by
a kind word, the word we failed
to give them the last time
we met.

Could it be that loneliness is there
        in that last word we left unsaid?

An old ghost might have an answer
        to that question.

When the old ghost comes again
        in that dream or
        pages of the book or
        humming the song of childhood,
        then we can ask,
        "What can I give you
        you do not already have?"

One day, you and I will be old ghosts.
        We must have an answer to
        that same question:
        "What can I give you
        you do not already have?"

19 May 2020
La Cieneguilla; Santa Fe, New Mexico

She Saw The Future Through The Eye Of Her Needle

The quilt.

She sewed when he was in the field
    with plow and seeds.

She sewed when he was in the barn
    with cows and horses.

She sewed when he slept without dinner.

She sewed, pieces of his denim shirts,
    his scent stitched into the seams.

She sewed, pieces of her flower-printed dresses
    from Blue Bird Flour sacks,
    fragments of their children's school clothes.

She sewed in her dreams.

She sewed in her memories
    of the children growing into men
    and women.

She sewed in the sour-milk of summer.

She sewed in the frozen calves of
    the ice-age winter.

She sewed in the acres of drought-dead
    cornfields.

She sewed in the horse struck by lightning.

She sewed the quilt to cover his casket.

She had sewed her body next to his body.

10 August 2018
Galisteo, New Mexico

Selections
by the Poet James McGrath

Selecting poetry from eight books of poetry published by Sunstone Press of Santa Fe, New Mexico, James McGrath, at ninety-four, reflects in the mud puddles of childhood, in the transparent grief of war and death, in the silver chalice of family and walking the dusty road. James looks through the cracked window of politics and the stained glass of the natural world, he shares a revisit in Ireland, Greece, Japan and Hopi. For poet, James McGrath, selecting poetry for his *Selected Poems* with fellow writers/poets in the digital-virus dominated life of the early 2020s is a brief pause on the journey.

From *At the Edgelessness of Light*, 2005

Son of the Hunter
  —*In memory of Francis Anthony McGrath, my father*

The deer hung his bronze head.
Dad stood me beside his bronzeness
    like a member of the family.

I let my picture be taken,
    my eyes wandering down his stretched
    hind legs tied with wire to the rafters,

my eyes wandering into the red opening
    that was once a hot stomach,

my eyes meeting the frosted stare
    of deer-eyes browned over
    with the last vision of pine-forest
    and rock-falls.

Even after the camera was put away
    and the hunters left the barn,
    my eyes continued to wander,
    to stop and stare
    at the great silence of coarse fur,
    the wide arching horns.

I wanted to crawl outside my eyes
    to curl up in the open circle
    of those wide horns,
    to be pierced as the deer had been pierced.

I wanted to feel the pain
    of that golden deer.

I wanted to run my teeth against
    the roughness of the horns
    as they entered his head,
    knobby and touched with his blood.

I wanted to be embroidered with his fur
    so I would never be cold again.

I wanted to animal,
    and I wondered how he cried
    when he fell off his mountain,
    and if I put my finger in the bullet-hole
    would he breathe again.

November, 1992
Santa Fe, New Mexico
Broadside self-published Fall 1995
Published 2003 in *Passager, A Journal
of Remembrance and Discovery,*
Mary Azrael and Kendra Kopelke, editors.

Ritsos and I
   —For Mary Lou Denning, my friend

Like Ritsos,
I want to hold my *briki* pot of coffee
        on top of fragrant dry twigs of thyme.
What coffee that will be!

I want us to row across the night bay of Panteli
        like Argonauts,
        Ritsos pulling on the right oar,
        me pulling on the left.

I'll carry my English-Greek, Greek-English
        dictionary with me.

I'll ask for translations of the moon-waves
        like bits of quartz bouncing on the aquamarine sea.

I'll ask for the words that say *blurp-blurp*
        to both of us
        as we dip our oars.

He will have his moustache running
        across his upper lip
        and along his mouth-edge to his chin.

Out on the waters there will be undulating splashes.

There will be a Greek word for undulating splashes.

I know we will gaze at the moon
        and see nothing,

Ritsos and I.

He will read poems to me in Greek,
        which I will understand
        without knowing a single word,
        like knowing what the moon says.

Ritsos will say,
        We've hidden inside each other.
No one will find us.
Only the moon on your
expectant lips . . . *

                September 2000
                Isle of Leros, Greece

Iconostasis of Anonymous Saints
by Yannis Ritsos, p. 261
Kedros Publishers, Athens, 1996

From *Speaking With Magpies,* 2007

There is a Magpie Inside Me
—For my daughter Jeni Keleen Viney

There is a magpie inside me
      next to the turtle and the dragonfly.

It speaks at odd hours.
      At night it awakens my dreaming foxes.

It flies to far-off places,
      holding clouds tight
      among its feathers,
      its beak carrying juniper berries.

It builds its nest in Spring
      before all snow melts.
      It listens to the seeping sounds
      of Winter weeping.

There is a magpie inside me
      next to the horse
      and the pterodactyl.

It waits, expecting hummingbirds
      to share their honey.

It preens its wings,
      making shining mirrors
      for iridescent beetles
      and star-eyed gnats.

It never sleeps.

It carries the sun from one horizon
      to the other.

It presses its head to my chest, it sings
      of loneliness and wild iris.

        12 September 2005
        Galisteo, New Mexico

A Week in the Round Tin Tub
—In memory of Uncle Nap and Aunt Sinnie

I was the last to bathe in the round tin tub
      on Saturdays. Aunt Sinnie added a bucket
      of hot water to what was already there,
      bringing the water up to above my belly-button.

On Sundays, when company came, two or three
      chickens were scalded in the round tin tub,
      leaving feathers stuck to the sides
      and sweet, thick chicken smells.

On Mondays, overalls, aprons, long-johns,
      two bottom bed-sheets were washed in it,
      rinsed in the river and hung up
      on the cherry tree branches to dry.

Tuesday night found the tin tub
      on the wood stove, boiling and sealing
      jars of peaches, green beans
      or piccalilli.

Wednesday might be the scrub-the-floor day
      when Uncle Nap and I had to stay out of doors.
      We usually went huckleberry picking
      or agate hunting on the Nuwaukum.

Thursday meant the tin tub was used
      to carry chopped wood. It had two handles
      so it was easy to carry to the woodshed
      next to the kitchen porch.

On Fridays, the tub could be used for most
         anything. I might sit in it for a haircut.
         Aunt Sinnie might shuck corn in it.
         Uncle Nap might mix up the pee
         from the pee-pots with water for the garden
         or make an extra big batch of slop
         and mash for the weekend to feed the pigs.

Whatever happened in that tin tub on Fridays,
         I had to bathe in it the next day, hoping
         the cake of Ivory soap was big enough
         to float and not get lost somewhere
         on the bottom.

                 10 March 2004

You'll Turn to Lichen
  —*For my poet friend Susan McDevitt*

In the ruins that press against the Burren
        of County Clare
        live spirits
        cloaked in lichens:
        white lichens for night,
        yellow lichens for day.

These ruins, open to the sky,
        send long trails of psalms
        through nettles in the graveyards:
        Come visit us. Come sit.

These ruins are welcoming places:
        open doorways,
        open windows with stone sills and lintels
        of carved cinquefoil and hazel leaves.

These are open abodes
        where silence lies in dark corners,
        where the Conleys, the Mahonys,
        the Keanes are voiceless.

Although there are wagtails and marsh orchids nearby,
        strangers do not linger long here.

An old man near St. Brigit's Well said:
        You mustn't stay too long
        in these places.
        You'll turn to lichen:
        white lichen at night,
        yellow lichen in the day.

                2 June 2005
                Ballyvaughan,
                County Clare, Ireland

From *Dreaming Invisible Voices*, 2009

Dog
   —*In memory of my Dog Year friend*
   Tadao (Rio) Suzuki

When I take my walks,
      I stop to listen to the voices
      of the world.

When I pause,
      I lie in shady places
      to feel the movement of the planet.

When I open my mouth,
      my tongue tastes the sweetness
      and sourness of the world.

When I doze easily,
      my ears open for you.
      I have many things to tell you.

Sometimes,
      sometimes when you touch me
      with your soft voice and your strong,
      kind hand, I think you understand.

I give you my loyalty and caring forever.

Even when you are angry and hurt me,
      I remain your companion forever.

Even when you are loving and hurt me,
      I remain your companion forever.

From *Valentines and Forgeries, Mirrors and Dragons*, 2011

My Winter Soldier

My brother played drums in his high school band.

He sang Bacharach songs to Fatima down the road.

He tickled my mother with a peacock feather.

He laughed at my 4th grade elephant jokes.

He teased Dad about his bright ties.

My brother came home last week from Iraq.

He wore a piece of shrapnel from his shoulder
      on a chain around his neck.

He had a prosthetic arm with five plastic fingers
      in a white glove.

He called Dad a motherfucker because he wore
      a tie.

He said he had shot elephants and peacocks
      in the Baghdad zoo for target practice
      with his buddies.

He said Fatima was just another stupid Hajji.

He sold his drums on e-bay.

Last night at dinner he told us how they poured
        gasoline on a library in Fallujah, shooting
        into the shadows until they ran red.

How the books burned; even Rumi couldn't escape
        the flames.

He cried in his room all night, tossed grenades
        of four-letter words into the dark.

This morning he never came down to breakfast.

18 March 2008
Santa Fe, New Mexico
Published in *Against Agamemnon: War Poetry*, 2009
Published in *Sin Fronteras: Writers Without Borders*, 2009

From *The Sun is a Wandering Hunter*, 2015

This is How I Walk

There are footprints in the sand
    that dance when the wind sings.

    This is how I walk.

There are trails between stones on the mesa
    left by foxes and coyotes.

    This is how I walk.

There are tracks on the branches
    of peach and juniper
    left by jays and bluebirds.

    This is how I walk.

There are pathways from yesterday to tomorrow
    left by ancestors.

    This is how I walk.
    This is how I walk home.

        15 July 2008
        Hotevilla, Hopi Reservation, Arizona

From *A Festival of Birds*, 2017

Your death

    and mine

    are but falling feathers

From *Mixed Greens*, 2019.

Song for The Daughters Buried in the Orchard

In Spring
      they are dressed in green, embroidered
      with the dew of morning apple blossoms.

In Summer,
      they sing with moon-night crickets
      leaving their songs of light
      in the nests of magpies.

In Autumn,
      when leaves fall
      across their shoulders,
      they weave memories into my hair
      with rosehips and horsetails.

And in Winter,
      when geese and robins fly South,
      there are red winged blackbirds
      who drop red patches
      onto their cheeks.

When the New Year comes
      flashing its promise of life
      across the orchard,
      they remain silent
      pulling love and sadness
      from my heart.

        1 November 2015
        Albuquerque, New Mexico

Taking Childhood to the Flea Market

The Little Orphan Annie cup
　　has finger prints on it.

The skate key has the dirty, knotted,
　　white string dangling.

One staring, brown-spotted glass eye
　　is missing from Teddy.

　　　"He's almost blind.
　　　Can he see me?"

I hear Winnie The Pooh sigh inside
　　The House At Pooh Corner.

　　　"Thank you for sharing
　　　so many cookies with me."

Voices get mixed up a bit now.

Tarzan of the Apes stays in his tree
　　gazing beyond the jungle
　　from his Big Little Book.

No one passing the table
　　hears the sound of Thumper
　　tapping his foot.

No one hears the weeping
　　of the Christmas angel
　　with the broken halo.

I was afraid to put *The Deerslayer*
     too close to the edge of the table.
     The war-hoops might scare
     inquisitive children.

No laughter from the pile of comic books;
     not even from the *Katzenjammer Kids*.

Perhaps some lovely lady past 86
     will pop-up at my table
     to cry over *Dick Tracy*.

I wonder what A.A. Milne would say
     about all of this:
     this childhood at the flea market.

He might not reissue *Now We Are Six*
     but write and publish *Now We Are Ninety*.

All I know is that my heart
     is bleeding sadness, memories
     and relief.

I only want the joy of these treasures
     to be seen-and-not-heard
     as I was.

          2 September 2015
          La Cieneguilla; Santa Fe, New Mexico

There Will Always Be a Poem

There will always be a poem
        in the corner of the room
        silent
        soft as a dust ball
        holding the echo of footsteps.

There will always be a poem
        moving across the wall
        with morning sunspots,
        golden words
        changing into shadows that hum.

There will always be a poem
        in the bread crumbs
        left on the kitchen table
        for lost ants to carry away
        into unseen holes in our hearts.

These are the poems unwritten
        by poets who use pen and ink,
        poems written under the breath
        when dogs sleep at their feet
        and cats hum on their shoulders.

Poems written without pen and ink
        are songs of curved-bill thrashers
        who shriek and lisp
        their brief stories
        between wild rose bushes
        and columbines.

Poems written without pen and ink
        are the open cracks
        in the bark of the apple tree
        reminding raccoons and robins
        not to leave behind
        any hints of falling stars.

There will always be a holy magpie
        looking into the heart of a poet.

        They hear the drumbeat of lost love.
        They hear the flute breathing of Spring coming
        when the poet will write another line
        of their love song
        that begins with the word home
        and ends with the word home.

If the poet waits for the moon
        to rise out of the lake,
        they will find their lines
        have neither commas nor periods.

In time,
        the poet will have written
        their love song
        in so many languages,
        the life-line in the palms
        of their hands
        will be the only map
        they can follow
        without getting lost.

This is to say,
        that poets write
        their unwritten songs
        between their mother
        and their father
        when there was no other place

to tell the world,
I love you.

    —James McGrath
    14 February 2018

    Published in *passager*, Winter, 2018/2019

From *A Temporary Silence*, 2019

I Considered Voting

I considered voting.
    I stepped under the cottonwood tree on the corner
    to be caressed by falling leaves.

I considered standing in line
    in my mask,
    in my state of full moon,
    in my state of migrating robins.

I considered the smile, the questions
    of the volunteer who asks,
    "Your name,
    your address,
    your undetermined heart beat?
    Did you vote before?"

I considered answering:
    "I am Jupiter. The shadow of a star.
    My address is the apple tree
    in the orchard at 83 Via de los Romero."

    "Yes. I vote every morning.
    I count the tracks of deer in my garden."

I considered using the black pen filling in
    those oblong shapes to darken my eyes
    to look like the woman killed
    on the street corner in Memphis.

I considered folding the election documents
    into paper cranes
    to toss around the election room.

"Yes. I am here to vote.
   I am joining the deer in the line
   just behind me."

   8 November 2020
   La Cieneguilla; Santa Fe, New Mexico

Drawing Pictures

In 1940,
in Berlin,
grandfather took my mother by the hand
to market for bread.
SS men grabbed grandfather.
He whispered to mother,
"Run. Hide in the potato sacks.
Do not go home."
Mother never saw her father again.

In 2018,
in Trenton,
father took me by the hand
to walk me to school.
ICE men grabbed father.
He whispered to me,
"Run across the street into the church.
Do not go home."

Today,
I sit with other boys and girls
in the church basement.
We draw pictures of our fathers and mothers.

31 January 2019
La Cieneguilla; Santa Fe, New Mexico

Nominated for a Pushcart Prize by *the kerf,*
College of the Redwoods, Crescent City, California, 2019

The Way Home

There is a well-worn, creased,
    sweat-stained map we carry
    in our silence.

X marking the place, the people,
    the thing that changed
    our life.

We may polish the gold
    of who loved us,
    tarnished from neglect,
    so they outshine the new moon.

We may wipe the dust
    from the place we hid
    our dreams, muzzling
    the scarecrow of childhood.

We may replace the street sign
    to the market where the farmer
    of watercress sprinkled
    rain water on our heads,
    baptizing us, Nesting Bird.

The map remains in the pockets
    of our open hands for us
    to read when the darkness
    is too dark, when we ask
    for the light from the eyes
    of our beloved to see,
    and it is given to us.

The map we carry in silence
      has no North, no South,
      no East, no West.

The map we carry in silence
      is the way home.

       11 March 2020
       Santa Fe, New Mexico

ABOUT THE POET

Poet, James McGrath, offers *Selected Poems of James McGrath* as his ninth book with Sunstone Press of Santa Fe, New Mexico.

James included the literary arts in his Columbia High School, Richland, Washington art classes in 1952-1955. His student, William Witherup of Seattle is an eminent Northwest poet.

He was Art Teacher as well as Arts and Humanities Coordinator for the US Department of Defense Overseas Schools in Germany, France, Italy and Ethiopia from 1955 to 1962. James held the same Arts and Humanities position with the DOD Overseas Schools in Japan, Korea, the Philippines, Taiwan, Okinawa and Midway Island from 1973 to 1985, when he retired the first time. During his tenure in the DOD Overseas Schools in the Far East, James inaugurated and edited *SUN, the Journal of Self Expression* for those schools. In twelve years, students and staff members had 3,256 of their literary, visual arts and musical compositions published and shared with their communities.

From 1962 to 1973, James was Creative Writing, Painting, Exhibition-Museum Arts teacher as well as Assistant Arts Director and Arts Director at the Santa Fe, New Mexico seminal Institute of American Indian Arts (IAIA). He was Dean of the College at IAIA from 1988 to 1990. In 2010, IAIA awarded James their Visionary Award.

From 1998 to 2014, James facilitated writing and visual arts in Santa Fe's Ponce de Leon Retirement Center.

In 1999, James began community poetry reading events in his orchard, which he continues today.

James was designated a Santa Fe Living Treasure in 2008. The New Mexico Literary Arts presented James their Gratitude Award in 2014 for his "Contributions to the Literary Life of New Mexico."

In 2015, the University of Baltimore's *passager's* editors, Mary Azrael and Kendra Kopelke, awarded him their 2015 Poet Award. *The kerf* of the College of the Redwoods in Crescent City, California nominated his poem "Drawing Pictures" for a Pushcart Prize in 2019.

James was United States Information Service, Arts America, Poet/

Artist in Residence in Yemen, the Kingdom of Saudi Arabia, and the Republic of Congo in the 1990s.

A biography of James, *James McGrath: In a Class By Himself,* by Jonah Raskin, author of *American Scream: Allen Ginsberg's "Howl" and the Making of the Beat Generation,* was published in 2012.

Previous community poetry sharings have included:

At Esalen, Big Sur, California: David Whyte, Sharon Olds.

In Abha, The Kingdom of Saudi Arabia: Ali Abdullah Marzuk, A. Al Quosi.

In Sana'a, Yemen: Ibrahim Mohamed Al-Attab.

In Brazzaville, Republic of the Congo: Marie Leontine Tsibinda.

In San Miguel de Allende, Mexico: Mark Doty, Alistair Reid, Marjorie Agosin.

At Listowel Writers Week, Listowel, County Kerry, Ireland: Nuala Dhomhnaill, Eilis Ni Dhuibhne, Marie Nyland, John McGrath.

At Hopitutqaiki, The Hopi School, Hotevilla, Arizona: Alicia Nequatewa, Mary Duwyenie, Jeanette Katoney.

On the Isle of Leros, Greece: Morgan Farley, Shama Beach, Margot Sheesley, Marcia Starck, Martha Yates, Dimitri Tsaloumas.

At Ballyvaughan, County Clare, Ireland: Morgan Farley, Enid Howarth, Shama Beach, Jeni Viney, Claire Mathey, Frances Hunter. A second time with David Whyte, John O'Donohue.

In Tokyo, Japan: Tadao Suzuki, Katsumaro Fukuzawa.

In the Philippines: Julius Prater, Jack DiBenedetto.

In India: Malathi Ramaswamy.

In Seoul, South Korea: Kim Hae Won, Yuen Won Sop.

In Bali and Ireland: Loretta McGrath and Tawnya Laveta.

In Albuquerque, New Mexico: Dale Harris.

In Santa Fe, New Mexico: Natalie Goldberg, Joan Logghe, Morgan Farley, Lonnie Howard, Criss Jay, Judy Toler, Wanda Gray, Janet Eigner, Jane Lipman, Susan McDevitt, Catherine Ferguson, Cynthia West, Elizabeth Raby, Michael Scofield, Julia Deisler, Craig Barnes, Marcia Starck, Mary McGinnis, Linda Whittenberg, and others not unmentionable.

Kate Shane, Santa Fe musician, frequently shares her Irish harp in the orchard during readings with James and other poets.

This is how the world rhymes with sharing.

PREVIOUSLY PUBLISHED POETRY

"Ode to a Frightened Sparrow." *America Sings 1949 Anthology of College Poetry*, National Poetry Association, Los Angeles, CA, p. 58, 1949.

"Vision Quest," "Painting By Indian Light." *Dacotah Territory*, Number 6, Winter 1973-74, Dacotah Territory, Editor James White, Moorhead, MN, pp. 22-25, 1974.

"Film Makers Reflections." *Arizona Highways*, January 1976, Phoenix, AZ, pp. 4-47, 1976.

"We Navajos." *Language and Art in the Navajo Universe*, University of Michigan Press, Gary Witherspoon, Ann Arbor, MI, pp. XVII, 203, 1977.

"As A Navaho." *Understanding Interpersonal Communication*, Scott, Foresman and Co., Richard L. Weaver, Glenview, IL, p. 51, 1978.

"Corn Legend." *Arizona Highways*, January 1978, Phoenix, AZ, p. 9, 1978.

"Tales of Uncle Nap." (4 poems) *The Best Man, Selections from the first three years of MAN!*, Mandala Publications Inc., Sharon Adams, Editor, Austin, TX, pp. 72-96, 1992.

"Child of the Hunter," "Somewhere Between The Kitchen And The Dining Room." *Enkidu Men's Poetry*, Mandala Publications Inc., Jeff King, Editor, Austin, TX, pp. 3, 18, 1993.

"This Pain," "Please," "Listening For A Voice," "When I Came Home From School," "Somewhere Between The Kitchen And The Dining Room," "When No One Was Listening." *In Cabin Six, An Anthology of Poetry by Male Survivors of Sexual Abuse*, Impact Publishing, Jill A. Kuhn, Editor, Big Bear City, CA, pp. 62, 67, 100, 118, 2000.

"There Is A River Running In The Blood Of Him." *The Cancer Poetry Project, Poems by Cancer Patients and Those Who Love Them*, Fairview Press, Karen B. Miller, Editor, Minneapolis MN, p. 8, 2001.

"Sometimes I Think Of The Death That Has Not Happened Yet," "Remains." *Inside Grief, Death, Loss and Bereavement, An Anthology*, Wise Press, Line Wise, Editor, Incline Village, NV, p. 4, 2001.

"Dear Old Friend Cecile." *Unsent Letters, Writing As A Way To Resolve And Renew*, Walking Stick Press, Lauren B. Smith, Editor, Cincinnati, OH, p. 84, 2002.

"Spring Cleaning." *passager*, Issue 36, Baltimore, MD, p. 5, 2002.

"On The Wall Above The Sea." *Mercy of Tides, Poems For A Beach House*, Salt Marsh Pottery Press, Margot Wizansky, Editor, Dartmouth, MA, p. 87, 2003.

"Speaking With Magpies." *Hunger Enough, Living Spiritually in a Consumer Society*, Pudding House Publications, Nita Penfold, Editor, Columbus, OH, p. 98, 2004.

"Son Of The Hunter." *passager*, Issue 37, Baltimore, MD, p. 28, 2003.

"The Lichens On Yeats Tower." *Bardsong, The Journal for Celebrating the Celtic Spirit*, Midwinter Issue, Volume 2, Issue 1, Ann Gilpin, Editor, Bardsong, Steamboat Springs, CO, p. 35, 2005.

"A Man Of Water." *Sacred Waters, Stories of Healing, Cleansing and Renewal*, Adams Media, Maril Crabtree, Editor, Avon, MA, p. 109, 2005.

"Drawing With Crayons." *Oracle, A Journal of Literary Arts*, Vol. 6, Brewton-Parker College, Mount Vernon, GA, pp. 48, 50, 51, 2007.

"Flying With Icarus." *Santa Fe Literary Review 2007*, Miriam Sagan, Editor, Santa Fe Community College, Santa Fe, NM, p. 87, 2007.

"In A Year Of Drought." *Sin Fronteras, Writers Without Borders Journal 12*, Las Cruces, NM, p. 44, 2008.

"The Genie." *Santa Fe Literary Review 2008*, Miriam Sagan, Editor, Santa Fe Community College, Santa Fe, NM, p. 80, 2008.

"The Tug Of Sun Pulling Up The Grass," "The Stone Walls Of County Clare." *Ballydonoghue Parish Magazine, 2009 Silver Anniversary Edition*, John McGrath, Editor, Ballydonoghue Parish, Lisselton, County Kerry, Ireland, p. 52, 2009.

"Self Portrait At 80." *Santa Fe Literary Review 2009*, Miriam Sagan, Editor, Santa Fe Community College, Santa Fe, NM, p. 101, 2009.

"My Winter Soldier." *Sin Fronteras, Writers Without Borders Journal 13*, Las Cruces, NM, p. 54, 2009.

"My Winter Soldier." *Against Agamemnon, War Poetry 2009*, Waterwood Press, James Adams, Editor, Huntsville, TX, p. 43, 2009.

"A Week In The Round Tin Tub." *Lavanderia, A Mixed Load of Women, Wash and Word*, San Diego City Works Press, San Diego, CA, p. 136, 2009.

"The Gate," "World I Love You." *Malpais Review*, Autumn 2010, Gary Brower, Editor, Placitas, NM, pp. 11, 12, 2010.

"A Space For Light," "Sky Of Reeds." *Reeds and Rushes Pitch Buzz and Hum*, Pudding House Publications, Kathleen Burgess, Editor, Columbus, OH, pp. 52, 78, 2010.

"Flying With Icarus." *Feast of Fools, Poems, Stories and Essays on Sacred Fools and Tricksters*, Sacred Fools Press, Melissa Guillet, Editor, Johnston, RI, p. 49, 2010.

"After The Snow Had Melted." *Santa Fe Literary Review 2010*, Miriam Sagan, Editor, Santa Fe Community College, Santa Fe, NM, p. 113, 2010.

"Crumpling The Paper," "The Real Thing." *New Mexico Poetry Review*, Spring 2010, Vol. 1, No. 2, pp. 50, 51, 2010.

"This Is What Happened In South Tacoma," "Bird," "The Poet Has No Place To Hide." *New Mexico Poetry Review*, Fall 2010, Vol. 2, No. 1, Kathleen Johnson, Editor, Santa Fe, NM, pp. 41-44, 2010.

"The Tug Of Sun." *Sin Fronteras, Writers Without Borders Journal 14*, Las Cruces, NM, p. 41, 2010.

"Dust," "Most Sell Home Call 986 6066." *Malpais Review*, Autumn 2011, Gary Brower, Editor, Placitas, NM, pp. 22, 23, 2011.

"Holly Berries," "This Is How You Praise The Land." *passager*, Spring 2012, Baltimore, MD, pp. 3, 62, 63, 2012.

"Directions For Walking In Mud," "Weaving On A Spring Morning." *Malpais Review*, Spring 2012, Gary Brower, Editor, Placitas, NM, pp. 26, 27, 2012.

"My Winter Soldier," "Dear Poem." *Lummox No. One*, RD Armstrong, Editor, San Pedro, CA, pp. 51-52, 2012.

"An Open Space For What Is Lost," "This Is Where We Come From," "When Life Breaks Down." *New Mexico Poetry Review, Centennial Edition*, Spring 2012, Vol. 3, No. 1, Kathleen Johnson, Editor, Santa Fe, NM, pp. 87-90, 2012.

"To Struggle With The Moon." *Santa Fe Literary Review 2012*, Miriam Sagan, Editor, Santa Fe Community College, Santa Fe, NM, p. 111, 2012.

"Weaving On A Spring Morning." *Sin Fronteras, Writers Without Borders Journal 16*, Las Cruces, NM, p. 48, 2012.

Featured Poet with 21 poems and interview. *Malpais Review*, Summer 2013, Gary Brower, Editor, Placitas, NM, pp. 22-67, 2013.

"The Archeologist As Full Moon." *Odes and Offerings, A Collaborative Exhibit of Poetry and Visual Arts*, The City of Santa Fe Arts Commission, Sunstone Press, Santa Fe, NM, p. 60, 2013.

"Never Given A Name," "The Color of Ice Melting," "Feeding The Fire," "Searching For A Reflection," "Anger And Confusion After Death." *The Disenfranchised*, Peggy Saphire, Editor, Baywood Publishing Company Inc., Amityville, NY, pp. 37-42, 2013.

"My Poems," "You," "Guns, Guns, Guns," "My Winter Soldier," "The Trumpet Player." Winner of 2015 *passager* Poetry Contest, Baltimore, MD, pp. 29-40, 2015.

"My Poems." *No, Achilles*, Waterwood Press, James Adams, Editor, Huntsville, TX, p. 38, 2015.

"My Poems," "The Trumpet Player," "The Dogs Are Barking." *Malpais Review*, Spring 2015, Gary Brower, Editor, Placitas, NM, pp. 153, 154, 2015.

"The Dogs are Barking," *The Gay and Lesbian Review*, November-December 2015, Boston, MA, p.47, 2015.

"10 January 2017." *Malpais Review*, Spring 2016, Gary Brower, Editor, Placitas, NM, p. 128, 2016.

"Drawing Pictures." *the Kerf*, College of the Redwoods, Crescent City, CA, p. 29, 2019. Nominated for a Pushcart Prize.

"There Will Always Be A Poem." *passager*, Winter 2019, Baltimore, MD, p. 78, 2019.

"Who Will Recognize Us?" "In The Silence of The Daily News Report." *Iconoclast # 121*, Mohegan Lake, NY, pp. 31, 38, 2020.

"Who Do I Ask?" *passager*, Winter 2021, Baltimore, MD, p. 143, 2021.

"birds sing one song please remember me," "Eight Things No One Can See." *The Deronda Review*, Vol. IX, No. 1. Esther Cameron, Editor, Efrat, Israel, pp. 6, 24, 2021.

"Honey At The Check-Out Counter." *Iconoclast #122*, Mohegan Lake, NY, p. 51, 2021.

"Where Do You Live?" *New Mexico Poetry Anthology*, Levi Romero and Michelle Otero, Editors, Museum of New Mexico Press, Santa Fe, NM, 2022.

"The Crow and The Lonely Child." *Iconoclast #123*, Mohegan Lake, NY, 2022.

"Tiepolo's Ceiling." *The Gay and Lesbian Review*, May-June 2022 Vol. XXIX, No 3, Boston, MA. p. 28, 2022.

"The Crow and The Lonely Child," "The Face." *The Deronda Review*, Vol. 9, No 2. Esther Cameron, Editor, Efrat, Israel, pp. 11, 39, 2022.

"I am Sending My Poems to Myself," "In the Book I Leave Behind," "Secrets At The Crossroads." *Glimpse*, Issue 55, Spring 2022, George J. Searles, Editor, Clinton, NY. pp. 39, 40, 41, 2022.

"In The Book I Leave Behind." *passager*, 2022 Poetry Contest. Mary Azrael and Kendra Kopelke, Editors, Baltimore, MD. p. 34, 2022.

Poetry in Films

American Indian Artist Film Series:
    Jack Peterson, Executive Producer,
    Tony Schmitz, Director,
    Don Cirillo, Cinematographer,
    Rod McKuen, Narrator,
    Poetry by James McGrath,
    KAET, Arizona State University, 1973 and PBS, 1974.
      "Fritz Scholder," Mission.

"Allan Houser," Apache.
"RC Gorman," Navajo.
"Joseph Lonewolf and Medicine Flower," Santa Clara Pueblo.
"Helen Hardin," Santa Clara Pueblo.
"Charles Loloma," Hopi.

Available through Archives, Institute of American Indian Arts, 83 Avan Nu Po Road, Santa Fe, NM 87507.

Editor of Poetry

Yearly Journal, *SUN*, for the US Department of Defense Overseas Schools in Japan, Korea, Taiwan, the Philippines, Okinawa and Midway Island, 1973 through 1985. Over 3,256 poems and visual art works by the students and staff of these elementary, middle and high schools. James McGrath was Arts and Humanities Coordinator for these schools, living in Tachikawa, Japan, from 1973 to 1976 and in Okinawa from 1976 to 1985.

Available at The Archives, The American Overseas Schools Historical Society, 704 West Douglas Avenue, Wichita, KS 67203-6104, www.aoshs.org.

Portfolio

A Crack In The Wall. Portfolio of 23 broadsides, James McGrath, poet, Manuel Yutuc, artist, printed on handmade paper by Juan S. Juan, Jr., Manila, The Philippines, through the courtesy of Fe Gonzales, Philippine Design Center, Manila. Portfolio latch of carabao horn and maguey twine. Baguio Printing & Publ. Co. Inc., Baguio, Philippines, 1981.

Twelve Poems. *The Source… The Image… The Journey.* Collaboration with Austin, Texas woodblock artist Daryl Howard. Annie Osburn, Author. Daryl Howard Art Inc., Austin, TX, 1990.

Ten Poems. *A Warm Stone To Dream Upon.* Collaboration with Austin, Texas woodblock artist Daryl Howard. Annie Osburn, Author. Daryl Howard Art Inc., Austin, TX, 2004.

Seven Poems. *Visions of Sonwai, Verma Nequatewa.* Collaboration with Hopi jewelry artist Verma Nequatewa. Annie Osburn, Author. Sonwai, Inc., Hotevilla, AZ, 2007.

Dreaming Invisible Voices. Collaboration with Santa Fe, New Mexico artist Margreta Overbeck. Sunstone Press, Santa Fe, NM, 2009.

Valentines and Forgeries, Mirrors and Dragons. Collaboration with Galisteo artist Catherine Ferguson. Sunstone Press, Santa Fe, NM, 2011.

The Sun Is A Wandering Hunter. Collaboration with Hopi artist Otellie Loloma. Sunstone Press, Santa Fe, NM, 2015.

Forty-eight Poems. *Master Reflections—Stories Between The Stones.* Collaboration with Austin, Texas woodblock artist Daryl Howard. Annie Osburn, Author. Daryl Howard Art Inc., Austin, TX, 2021.

www.ingramcontent.com/pod-product-compliance
Lightning Source LLC
Chambersburg PA
CBHW070344100426
42812CB00005B/1420